TADHG KENNELLY

UNFINISHED BUSINESS

TADHG KENNELLY

UNFINISHED BUSINESS

MERCIER PRESS
Cork
www.mercierpress.ie

Trade enquiries to CMD BookSource,
55a Spruce Avenue, Stillorgan Industrial Park,
Blackrock, County Dublin

ISBN: 978 1 85635 639 8

10 9 8 7 6 5 4 3 2 1

A CIP record for this title is available from the British Library

Printed and bound in the EU.

CONTENTS

Introduction

It is the most famous walk in Irish sport. The climb up the steps of the Hogan Stand at Croke Park on All-Ireland final day. All my life I'd dreamed about doing it. I'd seen footage of my father there, watched as my brother did it and now, here I was, about to do it myself.

I always thought it would be the happiest moment of my life but as I started up the steps I was gripped by sadness.

I did it Dad.

With every step a different image of my father came into my mind. There was him as a player, standing proudly in his Kerry jersey, 'The Horse' holding up the Sam Maguire as the winning captain thirty years ago to this day. There was him as a father, having a kick around with his two sons at the back of our pub. There was him as a caring parent, saying goodbye as his youngest son boarded a plane to start a new life on the other side of the world. Then there was him with the happiest smile I'd ever seen on his face as we hugged after I'd won the AFL Premiership with the Sydney Swans four years ago. Finally there was his funeral.

I did it Dad.

I knew I had to pull myself together. Our captain Darran O'Sullivan was giving his victory speech when suddenly my eyes were drawn to the crowd just off to the side of the stage.

There was mum. I quickly charged over, pushing my way through and over seats to get to her. I was crying, she was crying and we just looked at each other and hugged. No words were spoken. We just clung to each other as tightly as we could. She had been through so much, yet had soldiered on and basically held the family together. This win was as much for her as it was for me.

I did it Dad.

My sister Joanne was there as well and my auntie Breda, both also in tears, and I gave them a quick hug. I then saw my brother Noel and uncle Mikey up on the next level which unfortunately I couldn't get to, but the smiles on their faces said it all.

When I got back down to where my teammates were lining up – each player got the chance to walk up the steps to the stage and hold the trophy aloft – I knew what I had to do. My victory dance on the stage after the Swans won the AFL Grand Final had become sporting folklore. It had been an instinctive act, one which I did to send a message home to all my family and friends back in Ireland to show that I was thinking of them during the greatest sporting moment of my life.

That had now become the second greatest, as winning the All-Ireland final by four points over Cork in my first year back in the Kingdom, surpassed everything else that I'd achieved.

Mike Quirke was in front of me and I said to him, 'I think I owe this Irish crowd a bit of a jig.'

His eyes lit up. 'Yeah, do the fucking jig man. Do it,' Quirke said.

I told him that after he'd held up the trophy, to move it out of the way so I could get up onto the ledge. He played his part perfectly and as I stepped up, the crowd seemed to sense what was coming. As I started dancing, they went bananas. I then grabbed the Sam Maguire and thrust it up towards the sky.

That's for you Dad.

Chapter 1

'What the fuck is this?'

I had just been handed an Australian rules football for the first time and it felt really weird. For starters it was oval, not round.

'This is bollocks. What am I supposed to be doing with it?' I asked Danny Frawley, the coach from Australia who was handing out these silly looking balls to the rest of the Irish kids who'd been invited to the camp in Dublin. It had been set up by AFL (Australian Football League) club Collingwood, who were scouting potential prospects to take back to Australia. That sounded like a great idea to me: being a professional sportsman in an exotic location on the other side of the world.

However, my enthusiasm was taking a hit as I tried to get the stupid ball to bounce back to me. Looking around, it was obvious I wasn't the only one having trouble, with footballs bouncing all over the hall.

'Keep trying. You'll get the hang of it,' was Frawley's message.

He was right. The Collingwood coaches put us through a series of drills, including 1,500-metre runs and a lot of competitive work. It was hard but enjoyable, and the more I handled the funny ball, the better I was getting at it. By the end of the day the oval ball was at least coming back to me most of the time. To me that was enough. I was ready to become an AFL star.

A few days later my father and I met Frawley at Barry's Hotel in Dublin. He came bearing gifts, which I was very excited about – a bag of Adidas gear in Collingwood colours. They wore black and white and were called the Magpies.

Frawley didn't waste time, getting straight to the point. 'We are interested in getting Tadhg out to Australia on a contract,' he said. 'We're very, very interested, but we need to sort some things out at our end first.'

Dad was a bit shocked that his seventeen-year-old son was being targeted by a professional sports team on the other side of the globe. After a bit more discussion the time came for Frawley to leave, but he assured us he'd be in touch. I followed him to door. 'Don't forget, I want to play,' I said. 'I want to come to Australia.'

The first time I heard about Aussie rules was when I was ten and saw it on the TV show *Sports Daily*, which used to be on every Saturday morning. All I could really make of it was a lot of blokes with sleeveless tops kicking the shit out of each other. Later on I heard about the Irishman Jimmy Stynes, who'd gone over there and played for a club called Melbourne. He'd been very successful and had even won the medal for the best player in the competition. Also, a local Kerry lad named Seán Wight had gone over there in the 1980s and played 150 games. They were the symbols of the AFL in Ireland.

My interest in the foreign game heightened after I represented Ireland in the International Rules series against an Australian Under-17 team. Initially, I was selected to play for Munster against the Australians, who were playing matches against each province before a team was selected to represent Ireland in the final match. This was the first time an International Rules series had been played at a junior level. The seniors had been doing it for a few years, which had obviously increased people's awareness of the AFL in Ireland. The games, which involved a combination of Australian football and Gaelic rules, began in 1984 and continued in 1986, 1987 and 1990. However, there was then an eight-year gap before the concept of an annual series between the two countries at Senior and Under-17 level was established.

Despite Collingwood's promises, their interest, unfortunately, waned. I didn't really know what had happened. Carlton, another AFL club, had also spoken to me, but, again, nothing came of it, so my Australian dream quickly faded. Instead, I returned to focusing on playing with Kerry and finishing school.

I really hadn't given Aussie rules another thought until out of the blue we got a phone call the following year from Ricky Barham, the recruiting manager of the AFL club the Sydney

Swans. I was on my summer break having just finished my leaving certificate, and I had a job at the racecourse in Listowel, doing odd jobs and fixing up the place in preparation for the big race meeting in September. I had plans to do a teaching course at college in Limerick, but the phone call changed everything.

Sydney were conducting a try-out clinic at the Curragh, and Barham wanted me to be there, along with my parents, Tim and Nuala. The invite caught us all off guard, and we didn't know what to expect when we arrived at the Stand House Hotel, which the Swans had hired for the day. Out the back was a GAA pitch, so while the ten boys who'd been invited to take part went through their paces with Barham, the parents were entertained by another of the Sydney contingent, Basil Sellers. There were a couple of familiar faces there who had links to the AFL. Paul Earley was the first Irishman to go out to Australia to play Aussie rules, but he made only one appearance for Melbourne, in 1984, while Brian Stynes, the brother of Jimmy, who played two games for Melbourne in 1992, was also on hand to offer some advice.

The training went well, although that stupid oval ball continued to be a problem. They showed us the techniques for kicking and handballing, which was like a pass in Gaelic football but you had to hit the ball on the end with your fist and try and make it spin backwards. It was all very strange. I particularly enjoyed the marking contests, going up against the other kids, some of whom were monsters I'd never seen before, and trying to catch the football. While I might have been disadvantaged height-wise, I was able to make up for that once the ball hit the ground, and at one stage I even handballed it through the legs of one of the big kids who was about to grab me, then ran around and grabbed it and sprinted off.

After a brief lunch we joined the parents inside the pub, where Barham and Sellers conducted a three-hour question-and-answer session about Australia. They went through everything, explained how the game worked, told us that the AFL was made up of sixteen clubs all around the country, related something of the tradition and culture of Sydney and finished up with what the club offered. Everything was going smoothly until they went to the VCR.

What sounded like a good idea – showing a video-highlights package of Aussie rules – turned into a disaster. The highlights were made up of massive hits and bumps, with guys smashing into each other. I couldn't believe that this was what they were showing to try and win over potential recruits, and more specifically their parents. I looked over at Mum, and she was shaking her head. 'No way he is going over to that,' she said to my father, who also didn't seem too impressed.

At the end of the session we adjourned for some dinner, because the Swans wanted to talk to me and my parents after everyone else had left. Barham then called us into a room and dropped a bombshell. 'We want to offer Tadhg the scholarship to come out to Australia,' he said.

Even though I had been hoping that something like this would happen, hearing his words still hit me like a ton of bricks. I looked across at my parents, and they were similarly stunned.

'We would really like you to come over and have a crack at the AFL, because we think you've got all the attributes to make it,' Barham said. He then explained that it I was being offered a two-year scholarship, named after Ron Barassi, one of the greats of the Sydney club, and it would involve free accommodation and enrolment in an arts degree at the University of New South Wales. Every detail seemed to be covered, but my parents weren't satisfied and they started arguing with Barham about different things before Sellers called for a stop.

I would later find out that he was an extremely successful and wealthy businessman who was the club's benefactor. The only reason the Swans were in Ireland looking for players was because he was financing the operation.

'Hang on a minute,' Sellers said. 'There is one question I want to ask.'

He then turned to me and said, 'Tadhg, do you want to do it?'

I quickly nodded my head. 'Yeah, I want to do it.'

And with that all the arguing stopped. It was time for us to go, and everyone agreed to keep in touch. The Swans didn't need a definitive answer there and then, instead saying that they would be in contact shortly. The pre-season didn't start in Australia for another few months, so there was plenty of time to carefully consider the proposal. While I needed no time, I knew it was going to be a tough road ahead convincing my parents, in particular my mother. On the four-hour drive home that night, I perched myself almost in between them and started the campaign.

'I'm going. I'm telling you, I'm going,' I kept saying over and over and over.

'No, you're not,' my Mum said. 'Just sit back down or you can walk home.'

My parents didn't say much for the rest of the trip as they tried to process what had just happened. I knew it was a massive deal for them and that they were under a tremendous amount of pressure, given that I was the son of a Gaelic-football legend. Dad had won five All-Ireland titles with Kerry, captaining the team to its 1979 victory. Growing up, I had heard so many stories about what a great player he was, so naturally there was an expectation that his sons – my older brother Noel and I – would follow in his footsteps.

Up until that point I'd been doing that. I'd played in the Kerry Under-18 team at fifteen, something that had very rarely been done before, and then at sixteen I had been named Listowel senior team player of the year. And I had obviously played well for Ireland in the International Rules series, so my reputation was growing. Of course, being Tim Kennelly's son had a lot to do with the all the hype, and obviously the AFL clubs saw that and knew that at least I had the right pedigree.

But the thing that was driving me was the dream I'd had all through my childhood of being a professional sportsman. It was all I'd ever aspired to be. What a life: getting up each morning, putting on your football boots and going to training or a game. And you got paid! While I loved Gaelic football, it was only ever going to be an amateur sport, and I wanted the amazing lifestyle of a professional.

The fact that I'd already turned my back on an opportunity to pursue that lifestyle in England as a soccer player, was also at the back of my mind. I had played a lot of soccer when I was younger, representing Kerry at junior level, and I had been offered the chance to try out with two English teams, Tranmere Rovers and Crew Alexandra. Even though soccer had offered the lifestyle I craved, I decided it wasn't my cup of tea in the end and that chasing an All-Ireland medal was my calling.

Now Australian rules football had become my calling. I'd passed up one opportunity, I wasn't about to pass up another. Every day I would come home from work at the racecourse and after one step in the door say, 'Did they ring, Ma?' And almost every day Ricky Barham had rung.

We lived above the pub my parents owned, Kennelly's on William Street, and one day he rang and a customer answered the phone, which was situated in the bar.

'It's Rick from the Sydney Swans,' Barham said.

The local just grunted, went to the bottom of the stairs and yelled, 'Nuala, the bloke from Australia who wants to take your little boy away is on the phone.'

Every time I raised the subject with Mum, I got the same response: 'You're not going.' We would have massive arguments about it, which would generally end up with me slamming doors all through the house. Dad could see how determined I was, and behind Mum's back he actually encouraged me – but never in front of her. 'It's a great opportunity, you know. I'll talk her around,' he said.

Dad had done his research and spoken to a lot of successful sportsmen about my situation; for example, he asked Kevin Moran, who played for Manchester United, to look over the contract offer. He also spoke to a couple of his Kerry teammates, Mikey Sheehy and Eoin 'Bomber' Liston, who had been offered contracts to play soccer in England when they were young but had turned them down. They agreed that I shouldn't knock back such an opportunity, as they had done.

My plan was that I would go to Australia for just two years, and apart from being a great holiday and a great experience, it would make me a better Gaelic footballer. It was a win-win situation. I would get the opportunity to train in a professional environment, develop new skills and then return to Ireland a more complete footballer.

Eventually, after a couple of months of badgering, Mum relented. She jokingly said it was because she was worried about having no doors left on their hinges, given how much I was slamming them during our heated arguments. I think the bottom line was that she saw how determined I was and figured that if I was to go she wanted it to be on good terms, not bad. And I think she was banking on me not sticking it out for very long.

When word got out about the decision I was shocked by the harsh criticism that came my way. I was even branded a traitor. Everywhere I went, people would say, 'Why are you going? You've got everything here.' They wanted me to stay and lead Kerry to another All-Ireland final. 'You're going to be as good as your Dad,' the old timers would tell me.

Through all of this, my Dad was the shining light. He was miles ahead of everyone else in the way he thought, because he could have easily just said, 'No, my son is going to play for Kerry like I did.' But he understood where I was coming from more than anyone else.

One of the major factors behind my determination to seek something different was the fact that I felt as though my life was already planned out for me. At eighteen years of age I felt my path was set in stone: I would stay in Listowel, break into the Kerry senior team the following season and from there try and win as many All-Ireland medals as my father. Noel had broken into the senior team the year before, and I saw how he had to combine training three or four times a week with a full-time nine-to-five job. I knew if I stayed that was going to be me. I wanted sport to be my job, and that wasn't going to happen in Ireland.

In all the excitement of getting the green light, I soon realised I knew nothing about my new home. We finally managed to find a map of Sydney from somewhere and located the home ground of the Swans, the Sydney Cricket Ground (SCG). Something situated right next to the football ground on the map immediately caught my eye – Sydney Girls High School. I was going to heaven.

CHAPTER 2

Visa! What visa?

'What are you talking about?' I said to the lady behind the counter at passport control.

'You need a work visa if you are coming to stay in this country.'

I couldn't believe they weren't going to let me in after all I'd been through to get this far.

'I am here from Ireland to play for the Sydney Swans.'

I must have sounded convincing, because after consulting with several other people in blue uniforms she managed to find reference to a visa in my name in the computer system. Eventually, I was cleared to proceed into the promised land.

The last communication I'd had from the Swans provided me with a description of the man I was to meet when I got off the plane on the other side of the world: 'He will be a little bald man wearing a red jacket.' His name was Phil Mullen, and he'd been told that I'd be wearing a green tracksuit – I thought wearing the colours of my country was an appropriate look – although I was pretty sure he'd be able to spot the white, bright-eyed, skinny Irish kid amongst the pack of seasoned travellers.

I hadn't slept on the plane, as I'd been trying to get my head around the last few weeks of my life ...

The weather summed up the mood at home on 3 November 1999, the day that I left. It was bucketing down and was as miserable outside as it was inside, with Mum unable to control her tears, which was setting everyone else off.

It had been a big week leading up to my departure, as we'd had a massive party at the pub, with family and friends gathering for lots of singing and speeches. The popular Irish tune 'Many Young Men of Twenty' was sung over and over, with Listowel's famous playwright and author John B. Keane leading the way. Cards overflowing with money were thrust into my hand, as was the tradition when someone moved away – people's generosity was overwhelming.

It was an evening of reflection for everyone and I was certainly reminded of all the great times I'd had since entering this world upside down with my arse first on 1 July 1981. Maybe it was a sign of things to come, but I gave my Mum a torrid time during birth, and she haemorrhaged badly afterwards. I was always a bit different, even back then. I had blond hair as a little boy, while my brother Noel, who was one and a half years older than me, and my sister Joanne, who was one and a half years younger, were both red-heads. And in keeping with my peculiar ways, the only thing I would eat as a toddler was toast – nothing else.

One of my earliest memories was my first day at primary school. Noel was so excited to be taking his little brother to school that he got me up at the crack of dawn. Mum and Dad were still in bed, because they'd been working in the pub until early in the morning. Coolard National School was out in the country, so we had to catch the bus, although one of the teachers lived about a kilometre up the road from us, so we could sometimes hitch a ride with him. Noel dressed me in the dirty old clothes I'd worn the day before and off we marched to the teacher's house. When he was asked about the whereabouts of our Mum, Noel initially said, 'She is sick from drinking too many glasses of Harp.'

That was an interesting thing to say, given that everyone knew Mum hardly drank at all – only the odd glass of wine on a big occasion. Figuring his first attempt at a lie hadn't been a good one, Noel came up with another explanation: 'She's pregnant.'

Anyway, we got to school and were playing ball in the yard when Mum drove up in a panic. She'd already been to the school but hadn't spotted us and was about to go to the gardaí to report us missing. Adding to her anger was the fact our grandmother had knitted two lovely jumpers, both exactly the same, for her boys to wear on their first day at school together, yet here I was in filthy old clothes.

Noel and I were inseparable growing up. If we weren't at the pub, you'd find us up at the sports field kicking balls. All we wanted to do was emulate our father. After retiring from Kerry he played with Listowel, and we would be the mascots on game day and even train with the senior team, running laps with them and doing sit-ups and push-ups. Everything was football, football, football. We would watch the video *The Kerry Golden Era*, which showed Dad winning his All-Ireland medals, almost daily, and could recite the commentary from every game.

Living at the pub was perfect for us. Noel and I had our bedroom in the attic on the third level, and we basically did as we pleased up there, as Joanne and our parents were downstairs. The best part about it was that there was always something happening. People, often famous sports stars, were continually calling in to see Dad, and we could always go down to the bar and hang out, play pool or even serve drinks. We grew up very quickly in a pub environment, as we soon realised we had to have a quick wit about us. But the greatest thing about Kennelly's on William Street was its car park, which we turned into our own Croke Park.

Along the side of the pub was a massive wall with a small Carlsberg sign on it. That was our target – it was only about the size of a football – and each day we would have hundreds, maybe even thousands, of shots at it. Right foot, left foot, back to right foot and so on. If Noel hit it ten times in a row, I had to hit it eleven times. We lived out in that car park, which fortunately had a floodlight beaming over it, so we could be out there honing our skills at any time of the day or night, rain, hail or snow. We'd play matches with other kids and even the travellers would get involved from time to time, as they had to go past the pub to get to where they lived on the outside of town. In fact, I think the skirmishes with those guys actually hardened us up a bit as kids, because every time you played against them they'd try to smack you around.

My other love growing up was the farm. Listowel had a population of between 3,000 and 4,000 – with forty pubs, I might add – and the surrounding countryside was filled with small farming communities. The Kerry Group's milk factory was the lifeblood of employment for the town. At any opportunity I would go to my grandparents' dairy farm, and luckily for me it was on the bus route to my primary school. Often I would just jump off the bus if I saw any action going on down in the farmyard. A lot of my school friends lived out there, so sometimes I would just stay the night at my grandparents' – most of the time I wouldn't even tell my parents of my plans in advance – and then hop back on the bus again in the morning to go to school. I loved everything about the farm – being on the tractor or helping out around the place. Once I even tried to get out of hospital early when I was having my appendix removed because I knew they were cutting silage at the farm.

It was my love of the countryside that resulted in my first football controversy and gave me an early understanding of what it meant to have the Kennelly name. Even as young as seven years of age, the thing to do was register with your local club, and naturally I was signed up to play with Listowel. However, as my friends were out in the country, I was desperate to play football with them, so my grandfather also registered me with his local side, Cloumacon. It was an innocent mistake on his behalf, but it started a full-scale war, with Listowel outraged that the son of their greatest player was wearing different colours. Dad saw the funny side of it, although my Cloumacon career wasn't a very long one.

When we were older Noel and I went to St Michael's Secondary School in town, and it was very much a football school, given that the principal at the time was the assistant coach of the senior Kerry team. I also started playing a lot of soccer and doing athletics there. One of the great things about my father was that he never once told me not to play soccer or rugby or anything else. He never said, 'You are going to be a Gaelic footballer and that's it.' He didn't care as long as we were playing sports and loved what we were doing. I know a few of his old mates didn't look favourably on his offspring playing other codes, but Dad would happily drive us all around the countryside to soccer games or track-and-field meets.

However, I do remember one time when everything wasn't so rosy. There was a clash between a soccer and a football game, and I'd just had a fight with Dad, so to get back at him I decided to go down to the park to play soccer. The next thing I knew, Mum appeared in the car. 'Get in the car,' she screamed. 'You know your father will go mad if you're not at the game.' I knew he would, and although that had been my plan I didn't really want to play soccer, so I jumped in the car. Mum couldn't stop shaking her head and I knew I wouldn't be pulling that trick again.

I never did any athletics training, but I still managed to compete in numerous all-Ireland athletics finals from Under-10 upwards, including cross-country, with my best event being the 400 metres. My last all-Ireland final at the age of sixteen was my most memorable. I obviously didn't have a coach, and I was quite nervous before the race, so I decided to come up with my own tactics. They were quite simple – go flat out from the gun. It was an ambitious plan, but I figured I could pull it off. After 200 metres I was flying and even had the temerity to look around to see how far in front I was. I really should have known from previous meets that the proper way to run a 400-metre race was to conserve energy going around the bend and then let loose again. Not me, not today. I was off and gone and had the gold medal virtually around my neck at the 300-metre mark. Then, suddenly, everything changed. I couldn't move my legs. The lactic acid build-up had hit and I felt like I was going backwards. The last fifty metres took forever to finish as my competitors sailed past me, and despite a desperate dive I was just pipped for third. As soon as I crossed the line I hit the deck and started spewing up all over the track. I was in a world of pain. I couldn't believe I'd missed a medal.

When I got back to the car my father was sitting there smiling, looking as proud as punch. 'Ah, you just had a crack, didn't ya?' he said. 'You had a go at the start to see if you could last, and you sure didn't die wondering.'

I often wonder just how good I could have been with proper coaching, but as much as I loved running and playing soccer,

Gaelic football was always number one. And I had already experienced many memorable moments coming through the ranks. There was an extraordinary Under-13 final against arch-rivals Tarbert, a small town ten kilometres away from Listowel, which went to four matches. The first three were all draws, even after extra time. By the fourth match interest in the final was massive, and a couple of thousand spectators turned up. People were getting very carried away, and it became a major event for the two towns. One of our coaches was so fired up that he kept us in too long at half-time, so the referee threw the ball in without us on the field. Naturally, Tarbert scored a goal in our absence, but we prevailed in the end.

My first time playing at Croke Park was memorable, not because of how I played but because of how much I was shitting myself. It was an Under-18 All-Ireland final against Tyrone, and I was only fifteen. I couldn't sleep the night before the match and lay in bed seriously concerned about whether I would be able to kick the ball the next day. Thankfully, I did manage to score two points, but the game was a draw, and the replay was the following week back in Croke Park. Again, I was uptight before the match and this time I really let the occasion get to me. I was a non-factor in the proceedings and learned a very harsh lesson about playing on the big stage.

The other major disappointment of my junior career came in my last All-Ireland final. The Kerry Under-21 team played County Westmeath, a football minnow who rarely won anything. Noel was captain, and we were the overwhelming favourites because we'd swept everyone else aside throughout the season and had won the semi-final by twenty points. Again, I was taught a good lesson, as we'd clearly started to believe our own hype and were beaten by one point – we even missed a penalty – in one of the biggest upsets in years.

All those great memories were racing through my head when I boarded the plane at Shannon Airport with my father. He was coming with me as far as London and then I was on my own. I'd never been out of Ireland before, so to say I had no idea what to expect was an understatement. When we got to Heathrow Airport it was like the blind leading the blind, as Dad didn't really know what was going on either. We had to change terminals, and instead of getting a train or bus we walked and walked and walked. My suitcase felt like it had cement in it by the time we finally got to the check-in counter.

Our goodbye was short and sharp, because Dad didn't want to linger. By this time I was buzzing with excitement and couldn't wait to get on the plane for Australia, a trip that I'd been told would take more than twenty-four hours. A whole day in a plane! I couldn't get my head around that, and I suppose the smart thing would have been to sleep, but I was so worked up that there wasn't much chance of that.

There was a stopover in Singapore, but I didn't want to get off the plane, because I had no idea that this was normal practice. I thought when you got on a plane you were on it until you arrived at your destination. The flight attendants explained that we'd stopped for refuelling, so off I got and wandered around the transit lounge in a bit of a daze. I somehow managed to find my way back to the right gate for reboarding a couple of hours later.

I really didn't know what I was getting myself into. I had a vision that the Sydney Swans would be like one of the big professional soccer teams, such as a Manchester United or Liverpool, that I'd grown up watching in the English Premier League. There would be state-of-the-art facilities, with coaches and trainers on hand to look after your every need.

I was lost in my fantasy world when I saw it, my first glimpse of Australia. From the moment the captain on the plane came over the loudspeaker and declared we were starting our descent into Sydney, I had my face planted against the window. The closer we came to Sydney, the more shocked I was at the number of houses there were and how it was spread over such a big area. Someone had mentioned that Sydney was the biggest city in Australia, but it hadn't really registered at the time. It did now.

As soon as I walked out of customs and into the passenger terminal I saw the small bald man with the red jacket. We shook hands, and the man called Phil and I headed for his car. My mind was racing at a hundred miles an hour as I tried to take in everything on the drive towards the city. 'Shit, there is a lot of traffic,' I remarked.

Phil laughed and pointed at the clock on the dashboard. 'It's only 6.30 a.m. Wait another couple of hours and this will be at a standstill,' he said.

'You're kidding.'

I was starting to get an idea of the enormity of what I had got myself into, and in a weird sort of a way it made me even more determined to succeed. 'You know I'm not here for a holiday,' I said to Phil. 'I'm serious. I'm going to make it.'

Phil Mullen

'The day I picked him up at the airport he came out as large as life. One of the first things he said to me was, "You know I'm not here for a holiday. I'm serious. I'm going to make it." I'd known him for probably ten minutes and that was his attitude, which stood him in good stead the whole time he was here. He is probably one of the most determined people I have ever met. He knows what he wants to do, he knows when he wants to do it and he does it.

'He referred to the football as "a bit like chasing a rabbit" because it bounced all over the place and he couldn't get it. He spent hours and hours and hours just doing extra skill stuff. He was a great athlete, so he didn't have to really concentrate too much on that, it just came naturally, but the ball skills …

'I saw him have his first few kicks at the SCG, and they were average. But he just never gave up. Every time you would go to his house or something he would have a footy in his hand, and that reflects back on the fact that he had to make it, in his own mind he had to make it, and he just did everything possible to make it.

'The other thing about him is he made friends with everyone at the footy club. He's that sort of personality. I'm sure he made heaps of friends outside the footy club as well, but everyone looked forward to him being around. He was a breath of fresh air around the place. He would bounce in at a hundred miles an hour, and even when he was homesick he was still quite bubbly. Some people who get homesick are really down in the mouth, but he was still trying like hell to be as bubbly as he could.

'Everyone here says they miss him, because he was absolutely unique – certainly one of the most unique eighteen-year-olds I have ever met. At eighteen he was nearly as mature as he was at twenty-eight. He didn't change that much, and he was switched on. He was smart, and he was intelligent. He got his university degree and bought himself a house.

'He is just a unique character. I don't think in my lifetime I have met anyone quite as unique as he is. He's just someone special, and it's hard to explain in a few words what that means.'

Chapter 3

'You're probably going to have to get changed. Maybe put some jeans and shoes on.'

It was obvious that Cassie, the girlfriend of Jason Saddington, one of the Sydney players, had drawn the short straw. It was her job to tell me politely that I was dressed inappropriately for a night out in Sydney. I thought I was looking pretty cool in shorts and sandals, with the collar of my shirt pulled up, although, in hindsight, I probably did look like I was on holiday in the Canary Islands. I quickly retreated back inside and put on jeans and a t-shirt. We were going to a party at Jason's house, which he shared with another player, Leo Barry. They lived just around the corner from where I was staying in Coogee, a beautiful beachside suburb not far from the SCG.

The first thing Phil and I had done the previous morning after I'd arrived was go to meet my host family, Fred and Rachel Orr. They were an American couple, and Fred worked at the University of New South Wales, where we went straight away to get me enrolled. After that I got a whirlwind tour of the football club, and, to be honest, I was surprisingly disappointed. It was actually a bit of a dive. While the facilities were clearly way better than anything I had seen at home, they weren't exactly what I'd expected. The gym was downstairs in what felt like a dungeon, and all the offices were tiny. I guessed Manchester United's headquarters looked a bit different to these. I was escorted from office to office, meeting everyone I could, from the chief executive and receptionist, to the football manager Colin Seery and coach Rodney Eade, or 'Rocket' as everyone called him. I was also introduced to an assistant coach by the name of George Stone, whom I was told I'd be spending a lot of time with, as he had been designated the job of teaching me how to play Aussie rules.

Pre-season training started on Monday, so the Saturday-night party was the last chance for the boys to let loose before the hard grind began. There were a lot of players there and I was shocked at how much they were throwing back the beers. I had decided before I came out to Australia that as I was going over to play a professional sport, I was going to take things very seriously and not drink. Many Gaelic footballers won't touch a drink for the six months of the season, because they work their arse off, combining playing with a full-time job. I actually hadn't really done much drinking before, despite having lived in a pub and growing up in a country where having a pint was such a big part of everyday life.

My first experience with alcohol had actually been a disaster. I was fifteen and Mum and Dad had gone with Noel to Waterford, where he was receiving the *Irish Examiner* Player of the Year award. Rarely did both of my parents leave the pub, but because it was such a great honour they both wanted to attend. I had a couple of mates around and when my parents left I snuck downstairs and stole a bottle of vodka. None of us knew what we were doing, so we just started downing it straight. It wasn't long before we were all paralytic and couldn't stand up. My auntie Breda was taking care of the pub for the night, and she found me in the toilet hugging the bowl, throwing up everywhere. She then caught Joanne in the sitting room kissing a boy. It was chaos, and I pleaded with her not to tell Mum and Dad. Unfortunately, my pleas were ignored, and when Mum got home she flipped out. 'The one night I go out, I come back to find I have got a son who is an alcoholic and a daughter who is a prostitute,' was her memorable response.

As my first Australian party started to fire up I figured it was no good sitting in the corner drinking water and that I'd be better served by getting into it with my new teammates. It turned out to be the perfect bonding session, and by the time we hit the local nightclub I was flying. Two of the boys in particular, Ryan Fitzgerald and Heath James, took me under their wing and bought me drinks all night. They were drinking bourbon and Coke, but I couldn't stomach that so I had Malibu and Coke instead. I soon gravitated to the dance floor, where I enjoyed carving out a few moves. It was an awesome night and the perfect introduction to my new way of life, although I thought a bit differently about it the next morning.

The hangover was a ball-breaker. To top things off it was a hot morning, and there was no air conditioning in the house, so I was seriously sweating it up. My first training session was the next day, and I was desperate to impress from the start.

Holy shit. How am I going to do that now?

'Do you want to have a kick?'

The man who had been introduced to me as Mickey O was suddenly standing next to me. I had never met a black person in my life, so I really didn't know what to say or do. I would soon find out that the Aboriginal players were among the most skilful and exciting in the AFL, and Mickey O, real name Michael O'Loughlin, was one of the very best. But right then I wasn't concerned about the history of the Australian natives; right then I was shitting myself about having to kick that stupid ball in front of everyone.

'Yeah, all right,' was my equally daft response.

I could feel fifty sets of eyes looking at me as I tried to somehow get the ball to my boot and somewhere near Mickey O. I had never felt more embarrassed in my life. Thankfully, George Stone came to my rescue and called me over to him. He had a detailed plan about how we were going to approach my training, which he had spelled out in what basically amounted to a contract that I then had to commit to.

'This is what I will be accountable for, and this is what you're accountable for,' George said. 'I will teach you to play and all that, but you have to be diligent and do all the other things, like maintaining a high level of fitness, which means staying off the Guinness and out of our pubs.'

I laughed at his last point. Given how the weekend had gone, I figured I wouldn't be hitting the drink again any time soon.

He then handed me a document, which read:

> In order to play AFL at the elite level we (Tadhg, Colin Seery and I) agree on a clear understanding of what both parties would commit to':
>
> I would be accountable for:
> * Providing the right technique and skill programme
> * Supporting and driving the programme with a demanding practice schedule
> * Providing a six-weekly performance/progress review to all parties
> * Cultivating good habits: what to do (game sense); how to do (fundamentals); want to do (desire)
> * Empathy in regards to Tadhg's relocation from his homeland and wholesale changes in his life
>
> Tadhg would be responsible for:
> * PMA (positive mental attitude)
> * Diligence and perspiration
> * Repetitive practice
> * Maintaining a high level of physical fitness
> * Paying attention to diet, rest and sleep
> * Setting key skill goals
>
> All parties agree to the 'Patience, Persistence and Perspiration' clause.
>
> There is no 'how to' guide to being an elite AFL footballer, and both parties need to understand the task ahead. In essence it will be very difficult, but with the appropriate support and

encouragement we might be able to unlock the potential Tadhg has shown in the GAA and make him into a player who could play at senior level for the Swans. That is, 'build the perfect beast'.

Feedback to stakeholders:
1. Family back in Ireland – very important
2. Swans board – Ron Barassi Scholarship
3. Basil Sellers
4. Coaching panel
5. And sincere and specific feedback to Tadhg

Reading the document made everything clearer. This was a serious business.

There was also a performance plan that went with the contract. I would be assessed in three categories: 1. fundamentals (kicking, handballing, marking, tackling, etc.); 2. tactics (set-plays, tagging, positional play); 3. game sense (game and matchplay format). At the end of my first six weeks I would receive my first report card.

'The beauty is, Tadhg, you're a blank canvas,' George said. 'We can start from scratch.'

The priority was the kicking. According to George, that was the key as far as Rocket was concerned. If I couldn't kick, I wouldn't get a game for the Swans. The problem for me was that in Gaelic football you kicked around the corner, meaning you swung your legs across your body all the time. The round ball allowed you to make contact with it at different angles so more often than not you weren't running straight at your intended target. Everything about Aussie rules was about running straight and dropping the oval-shaped ball straight onto your boot. To overcome this we stripped the art of kicking back to its basics. George made me stand on my left foot with my right knee bent and then kick the ball without taking a step into it. This was all about getting the drop of the ball right, because given that it was an oval shape there was more room for error than with the round ball. When I progressed to stepping into the kick George put me alongside the fence on the outside of the ground, which stopped me from following my natural instinct of going around the corner. If I did, I would get a nasty whack to my shin.

It was tedious stuff, but every day there was a new challenge or a new drill. Instead of the fence we would use flexible flag sticks, like the ones used in slalom skiing, where you would smash into them but they'd continually bounce back upright. My aim was not to even touch the line of flag sticks while I kicked the ball. We'd also practise next to the goalposts, anywhere that it was hard for me to go with my natural instinct of swinging my leg around the corner. We focused mainly on my preferred right foot, but also did work on my left. In Aussie rules you need to be able to use both feet, as you have opponents coming from every side trying to tackle you and stop you from getting a kick away.

When I joined in with the main group I would try to avoid kicking and handball whenever I could. There was certainly no holding back for the Irishman! I was thrown in with everyone else for the main skills session of the day, usually in the morning, and then in the afternoon I'd do a weights or running session and then another two hours of one-on-one skills with George and Dougie Atkinson, who was the team manager, at the ovals at Randwick Army Barracks, where we did all of our pre-season training.

While learning how to kick was the priority, there was also the minor matter of being able to pick the ball up. Seriously, chasing an Aussie rules football *is* like running after a rabbit. You know how rabbits zip about all over the place, changing direction at the blink of an eye? Well, that's exactly what the oval ball does. Its bounce is quick and unpredictable, with no rhyme or reason as to what direction it goes in. I used to look on in awe as the other players watched the ball in flight and generally knew what it was going to do when it hit the ground. I had no idea and consequently spent hours running around like a lunatic trying to grab hold of it, much to the amusement of anyone watching.

One of George's early observations was that I needed to put on weight and quickly. I was seventy kilograms, if that, and when he introduced me to tackling drills I quickly understood why he wanted me to bulk up. I was shitting myself every time we did a tackle drill simply because I had never experienced anything similar before. While there was some physicality in Gaelic football, with big hits here and there, I was never worried about being piledriven into the ground with my arms pinned by my side. That's tackling in Aussie rules.

I was never really shown any specific technique for tackling; again, it was more of a case of getting in there with the group at training and learning on the job. It didn't take me long to realise Rocket was a tough nut, and his philosophy to tackling was simple: 'Just get hold of the fucker and get him on the ground. And don't get caught yourself.' The second part of his dictum came easier to me, because I was extremely quick and agile, and with my light frame I was able to avoid getting tackled quite a bit.

The other part of the game I struggled with was marking. I was continually bumped or manoeuvred out of the way because I wasn't used to contact in marking contests. The Gaelic way is to have two players charge at the ball in the air, with the rules stating that you can't shoulder them, bump them early or push and shove them under the ball. In Aussie rules it's all about using physical strength to get your opponent out of position – within reason, as there are rules against blatant pushing or grabbing. It's actually an art form, and I soon realised that it was going to take me a long time to perfect it.

While the practical side was extremely difficult to master, the theory side was even more confusing. I arrived knowing absolutely nothing, so George had to fill me in on the basics of the game. He told me that there were four quarters to a match, each running for approximately thirty minutes. There were four posts at either end, two big and two small. The big ones were the goalposts, and if the ball was kicked in between them, it was called a goal and was worth six points. If the ball was kicked between the goalpost and the small post, this was a behind and was worth one point. There were two umpires in the middle of the ground who controlled the game using whistles, while there were also boundary umpires who ran around the outside line and threw the ball back over their heads when it went out of bounds.

He also explained that there were sixteen teams in the competition, ten of those in Melbourne, which was the traditional home of the AFL. The rest were spread across the country, with two teams in Western Australia, two in Adelaide, one in Brisbane and one in Sydney. There were twenty-two rounds in a season, with the top eight teams playing off in the finals, which had a whole system of its own.

George had a number of videos to illustrate his points. He also tried to explain the rules on a whiteboard, which was like learning a foreign language. I understood you weren't allowed to tackle people without the ball, and pushing and grabbing in marking contests was a no-no, but that was only the tip of the iceberg. After ten minutes I put up my hand. 'George, I don't know what the fuck you are talking about,' I said.

We agreed that the only way I was going to learn was by playing, which would happen when I returned after the Christmas break.

The other area I had to get up to speed with was the lingo. In one meeting Rocket had said, 'Bomb it long down the guts.' I hadn't a clue what he was talking about. It was later explained to me that he meant to kick the ball long down the centre of the ground. There were plenty of other examples of Aussie slang that I had no idea about; for example, 'Yogi Bear' referred to your hair, so people would say, 'Your Yogi Bear looks good today.'

The first six weeks really flew by, and while it had been a shock to the system the major bonus was the suntan I'd acquired. Unlike a lot of Irish people who have red hair and pale skin – such as Noel and Joanne – I have olive skin that turned dark brown when exposed to the sun, which was every day in Australia. I knew everyone would freak out back at home when I rocked up looking like a rock star with my new tan.

At our final meeting before I was scheduled to get back on the plane for the long journey home for Christmas, George showed me my first performance review. All the key learning areas had been broken down into specific exercises, judged in categories: no improvement, slight improvement, general improvement and good progress. Thankfully, there were no ticks under 'no improvement', with the majority in the 'general improvement' and 'good progress' columns.

George's comment read:

> Tadhg is further advanced in skill developments, and his adaptation to the oval ball has been impressive. At the end of the six week pre-Christmas programme Tadhg's work ethic and willingness to learn is above expectations, and progress in the key learning areas is above expected targets. An area of concern is his light frame, which will need further development

> on a rapid scale in order to meet the body-contact demands of Australian rules. However, he remains positive and eager to learn.

It then listed the amount of hours that we'd dedicated to my programme. I had done a grand total of fifty-three hours, which was broken down into specific areas: general training sessions (ball work, running) thirty-six hours; individual training sessions (marking, kicking, handball) eleven hours; and video/whiteboard sessions (game sense, tactics, rules) six hours. This didn't include weight training, swimming, or recovery and massage sessions, which were all part of the pre-season programme.

After digesting the contents of the report I looked up at George and told him my simple aim in life. 'I just want to play one game, George. I don't want to play 100. I just want to play one game of AFL football.'

Chapter 4

'What is your name?'

The ambulance officer was leaning over me, trying to work out if I was in control of my senses. 'Tadhg Kennelly,' I said.

He looked over at his partner and frowned. 'Spell it.'

'T. A. D. H. G.'

This didn't help matters, as I sensed they were now convinced I was out of my mind and were explaining as much to a couple of the Swans people, including the captain Paul Kelly, who had gathered around the ambulance. My accent had already caused me problems. People kept asking me to repeat things, and I had to coach them how to pronounce my name. I'd say it was 'Tige', as in 'tiger' but without the 'er'.

'Nah, that's his real name,' I heard Kelly say. 'He's Irish. He's not out of his tree. Seriously, his name is Tadhg.'

This comical scene was taking place because about twenty minutes earlier I'd collapsed during a six-kilometre run around Sydney's Centennial Park. In hindsight it was complete madness that I was even training, given I had only arrived back in the country that morning after my plane had been delayed at home because of snow. So, after a couple of weeks of drinking and partying hard back in Ireland, where it was freezing cold, I'd spent more than twenty-four hours on a plane and then gone straight into training session in the heat and humidity of Sydney at the height of summer in early January. Crazy! We'd even done a half-hour skills session before the run, and I'd actually started getting a bit light-headed and dizzy during that but had decided to soldier on.

I was three-quarters of the way through the run when suddenly I hit the dirt. I was obviously badly dehydrated and had fainted, falling face down onto the path. When I came to, George and Steve Malaxos, one of the assistant coaches, were propping me up against a tree.

'Shit, I've killed the Irishman,' George was saying.

'Maybe I should go and get some water out of the pond,' Steve suggested.

'You're kidding! That stuff is septic. That will definitely kill him,' George barked.

They managed to hail the park ranger, who drove us back to the club, where Colin Seery was waiting for us. He'd called an ambulance and didn't look happy. 'I'm going to have to ring his parents and tell them we've nearly killed their young fella,' he said to George, who was explaining how I'd literally bitten the dust.

The club's medical staff had been trying to pump red Powerade into me to get my sugar levels up, and it was splashed all over my shirt, which gave the appearance that I'd been bleeding. This further intrigued the already confused ambulance officers. Eventually, they took me to hospital and put a drip in my arm. I stayed overnight, and the first person to visit was Seery, who was shitting his pants about what had happened and even offered to have me stay at his house for a week to help with my recovery.

If any good was going to come from the incident, at least I knew I'd never have to get off a plane and go straight to training again. It was going to buy me a few days off down the track.

Getting back on a plane was all I could think about for the next three months as I was hit by a serious bout of homesickness. Every time I was at my local shopping centre I was drawn to the Travelworld, which was on the left-hand side as you went down the escalator. I would stand there and stare at the fares for London and picture myself walking inside and booking a ticket. So many times I wanted to do it – just hand over the $1,500, not tell anyone, hop in a taxi to the airport and ring George when I was back home in Ireland.

I was in a very dark place; in fact, I would say I was depressed. Each night I would cry myself to sleep. I would hide in my room and ask myself over and over again, 'What the fuck am I doing?' I told no one how I felt. I stopped ringing home because I found that when I spoke to Mum or Dad it actually made me feel worse, and I also didn't want them to worry. I am generally an upbeat sort of person, and I continued to try and maintain a positive façade, hiding my real feelings from the world. A lot of that was because of embarrassment. I would often scream at myself when I was lying in bed, 'Don't be a fucking girl.' But I couldn't help it. The tears wouldn't stop, and the feeling of helplessness wouldn't go away.

The problem was simple: I was out of my comfort zone. All my life my comfort zone had been the football field. If there was anything going wrong in my life, if something bad had happened at school or at home, it would disappear the moment I got on the football field. That was where I was in total control, where I was the most comfortable. However, when I came to Australia I wasn't just in a totally different environment off the field, I was also in a totally different environment on the field. I was lost, like a lost puppy. I really had no place where I was comfortable. I couldn't disappear into my own world on the field, because that comfort zone wasn't there any more. I didn't have one. I had nothing.

What I did have a lot of were doubts about whether I was good enough to play AFL football. What had I been thinking? That was just the problem: I hadn't really thought about how difficult it would be to travel to the other side of the world and try to master a completely foreign game. I now seriously didn't know if I could do it.

Thankfully, slowly but surely, the dark fog in my mind started to clear. The one thing that kept me from getting on the plane was a fear of failure. I didn't like to let people down, particularly given that so many had gone out of their way in Sydney and back home to give me this unique opportunity. Most importantly, I didn't want to disappoint my father. The simple fact, which was becoming more and more apparent to me, was that I didn't want to go back to Ireland having not played a game of AFL football.

My training had a lot to do with the brightening of my outlook, which was starting to improve and giving me hope that I wasn't wasting everyone's time. I was also starting to make some good friends, in particular a couple of fellow rookies in Paul Allison, who was from Tasmania, and a local fella named Scott Muller.

Whereas GAA teams have panels, the AFL has a list. A senior list usually has thirty-eight players on it, with a handful of players on what is called the rookie list. Being on the rookie list means you have to wait for a spot on the senior list to open up, usually through a long-term injury, before you are elevated and eligible to play senior football. I was called an international rookie and was bound by the same rules.

Anyway, I began hanging around with these two guys, and one weekend they decided to bleach their hair, so I thought I'd do the same. A blond-haired Irishman was something a bit different, and I thought I looked pretty good until Rocket took aim at me. I was having a laugh with a couple of the boys before the start of training when I heard a voice from behind me say, 'You're not here for a fucking holiday, are ya?'

I froze. Nothing came out of my mouth as I watched the senior coach turn and walk away. I grew up in an environment in which you read a lot into whatever the coach said, and you always did what he said. You respected your elders and did everything to keep the head coach happy. That night, the first thing I did when I got home was grab the clippers and shave off my blond hair. Later on the club also had a quiet word with me. They didn't want me hanging around with my two new friends, as it was hinted to me that they weren't going to last very long at the Swans.

My career didn't look as though it was going to go too far, either, after my first-ever game of AFL football lasted just ten minutes. I was really nervous in the lead-up to the intra-club practice match, but George insisted that I should just run around and enjoy myself. But I still had no idea what I was doing, and injury brought a quick end to my debut game. I had gone up to take a mark, and when I came down I landed on my teammate Brad Seymour's foot, rolling my ankle badly. I hobbled off and took no further part in the game.

As much as training and playing was important, watching was also a critical tool in my learning process. My first impression when I sat and watched a full game was that it seemed a bit slow. How wrong I was! The constant stoppages, which Sydney thrived on, were deceiving. A stoppage occurs when a player is tackled, the ball is in dispute on the ground and no one is able to clear it. The umpire is then forced to come in and throw the ball up to try and clear the congestion, with the two ruckmen contesting for the ball in the air and trying to tap it to the advantage of their teammates.

I didn't realise until I was actually out there the speed with which the ball and the players moved and the physicality of the sport. Every game I watched with George I'd ask questions about anything and everything. I also got a chance to travel to Melbourne with Rocket and George to watch a couple of games at the MCG (Melbourne Cricket Ground), which was the mecca for AFL football. Living in Sydney, I didn't really grasp how big the game was and what a religion it was in Melbourne. There are more than four million people in Sydney, but the majority of them are rugby league fans. All you read about in the papers is rugby league, with the AFL maybe getting half a page. The Swans were originally from South Melbourne until they relocated up north in 1982, and in many respects they were still battling to be accepted into what was essentially a scene dominated by another sport.

One of the games at the MCG featured the Brisbane Lions, and the coaches wanted me to watch Nigel Lappin in particular, as he was the type of player they were trying to mould me into. I took notes and was blown away with the amount of work he did, the volume of his running and the ground he covered. If that's what they were expecting from me, I had a long, long way to go.

For the previous six months, I'd taken an Aussie rules football with me everywhere I'd gone. When I was sitting on the couch at home watching TV it would be in my hands. If I was going to the shops, I'd have it with me, and the boys would say, 'Man, that's not cool.' But I didn't care. I was taking that footy everywhere because I needed to feel as though it was an extension of my body in a way.

I had started chipping away, playing for the Swans reserves team. They played in the local Sydney Football League, which was a bit of a joke, because we won almost every game by twenty goals. Professional footballers versus amateurs in a non-football town equalled a significantly lower standard compared to the reserves competition in Melbourne. I even kicked five goals in one match – even though I was still kicking around the corner – which I was pretty excited about, and after each game I would sit down with George and watch a video of my performance. Every now and then he would say something that would give me a kick along. In one particular game I sidestepped an opponent. Then just as I was about to kick the ball, another dived in front of me, and I instantly pulled back, letting him fly in front of me, and then ran forward again to deliver the ball into the forward line. It was a move I'd done hundreds of times in Gaelic football, but it certainly got me some loving from the coach. 'You will play league football,' George declared.

Wow! That was the first time I had heard him say such a thing. Something that simple had convinced him that I was on track to achieve what for most of the past year had seemed impossible. From that moment, my confidence soared, although there was a hiccup on the home front, which I found out about after being summoned to Phil Mullen's office.

'We need to talk,' Phil said, with a very serious look on his face. He'd just received a visit from Professor Orr and his wife, who'd suggested it might be time for me to move out of their house. The problem centred around my relationship with their daughter. I pleaded innocent on the account that the daughter was several years older than me, but it didn't seem to wash, and I soon packed my bags. This wasn't ideal, and I briefly crashed with Daryn Cresswell, one of our most experienced and best midfielders, and his family, before bunking down with a couple of other teammates, Jared Crouch and Gerard Bennett.

While the Olympic Games coming to Sydney in 2000 was obviously a massive event for Australia, the exciting part for me was that the AFL had brought forward the end of its season. This meant that I would be going home at the end of August, a month earlier than normal and in time to watch Noel play in his first All-Ireland final for Kerry against Galway.

It was a cracker of a final, with the game finishing a draw. This meant that we had to return to Dublin a week later for the replay, which Kerry won. It was huge, and I went on a bender with three of my mates from school to celebrate. When you win the Sam Maguire cup, the tradition is that for the next week the trophy spends each night in a different town of the winning county. We followed it all the way back home, getting pissed every night and sleeping in our car. It was a fantastic time and a great way for me to celebrate what had been the most remarkable year of my life.

Noel Kennelly

'He always had this drive and determination growing up. Straight up it was like, "this is what I am doing", and no one could change his mind. If he wanted to finish the game, the game was finished. There wasn't an extra ten minutes or anything. When he made his mind up that was it, so when he made his mind up about Australia it was always going to be the same thing.

'He'd been in the Kerry minors and was earmarked to go straight into the senior team, and initially we thought he was going to go to Australia for just two years. It wasn't like, "I'm going for ten years and I'll see you when I'm twenty-seven." But he did so well out there that he just gathered momentum and got better and better. He was a big loss, especially for the club here in Listowel. It was massive to lose a player with his talent for ten years.

'My first trip to Oz was in 2003 when I went out there to have a groin operation. It was in the February, and in Ireland it would have been minus two with snow, wind and rain. I went straight to Sydney, and it was stinking hot. I stayed with Tadhg. He had two double beds, and we put a fan in between us on a swivel chair because there was no air conditioning in the house. I'd wake up in the middle of the night, and there would be sweat pouring down my face, so I'd kick the chair so it would swivel back and the fan would be on me again and I could go back to sleep. Next thing, half an hour later, I'd wake up and the fan would have been kicked back to his side. This went on all night, so the next day we went a bought a second fan, because there was no way we were doing that every night for the next six weeks.

'I really loved Australia: the sun, sea, beach and lifestyle, with everyone having barbecues. It's such a sports-orientated country, and you can get out in the open and go for a run or do something every day because the weather is fabulous.

'Tadhg used to bring an Aussie rules ball home with him, so I got used to it, and the coverage in Ireland over the last five years or so has been massive. I think it's a great game, a very fast game, with good hits and great skills. The oval ball is the biggest problem for a Gaelic footballer, but once you master that they are very similar games – the skills in both games aren't too different.

'The Grand Final was unreal. That last quarter, I knew there were four twenty-minute quarters with some extra time, but we were like, "C'mon, blow the horn." There was something like an extra ten minutes in that quarter, and it was amazing for Leo Barry to catch the ball, and Tadhg was right there holding onto his opponent's jersey. Afterwards we got into the changing-room and had a beer with him. It was a golden moment, especially given what happened a couple of months later.

'Australians don't understand where he came from to get to where he did. They don't understand the sacrifices he made to get there, what it means to pluck an eighteen-year-old out of a secure environment of family and friends and stick him in Oz on the other side of the world. It's an amazing achievement. If he hadn't won a Premiership, he might still be out there trying to win one. It's a lot easier to play if you're well liked, and the Swans fans took him to heart, which was great.

'When Dad passed away, I had to tell Tadhg. It's the hardest thing I've ever had to do – to tell my brother, who was so many thousand miles away, that his father had died. I couldn't console him, and my words just went in one ear and out the other.

'Towards the middle of last year (2008) I figured he was going to come home. His heart wasn't in it any more. When he finally made up his mind I think the hardest part was telling the Swans, telling the players and the management, who he had such a bond with.

'It's been great having him back. It was easy for him to get straight back into football over here, because the pace of the game isn't as fast. But it's been amazing having him around, to be able to go for walks together and talk about games and stuff.

'We were actually remembering one of his funniest moments the other day. It was when he was in the Under-13s, and some teams had girls playing to make up the numbers. Listowel were losing by two points and Tadhg was trying to get a goal to win the game. Anyway, a girl tackled him and pulled him to the ground, like an Aussie rules tackle. Then she got up and was running away when he kicked her in the arse. He was sent off straight away. It was very, very funny.'

Chapter 5

'Don't fuck me about. Is he going to make it or is he not going to make it?'

My father was leaning over the table, glaring at George. 'If he is not going to make it, then we've got bigger fucking fish to fry than this.'

We were in George's office. I was sitting next to my mother and father on one side of the desk, while Rocket was alongside George, who was looking a little bit uncomfortable. I rolled my eyes at Dad. My father was an intimidating character, especially because of his powerful build – hence his nickname 'the Horse' – and I had seen him do this many times.

'I think he is going to make it,' was George's careful response. 'I think he can be an AFL player.'

'Well, if you think he can be a fucking AFL player, then he can stay, but if you don't think he can be a fucking AFL player, then he is coming home now.'

George quickly backed up his earlier statement. 'I am pretty sure he can make it.'

And with that my father stood up and said, 'That's good, George, that's good. We'll let it go at that, then.'

He walked out of the office. Mum and I quickly followed, but I managed to give George a big smile and nod of the head. He'd done all he had to do – put my father at ease for the moment.

It was Easter 2001, and my parents had come out to see how I was surviving on the other side of the world. The timing of Dad's questioning was perfect, because for the first time since I had arrived eighteen months before I was convinced I would make it. This belief had all come about after just one game.

The Swans had played a pre-season match against Collingwood in Newcastle, which was about an hour away from Sydney. I was originally selected to play in the reserves' game, but only played a half before they pulled me out and put me in the seniors. This was allowed because it was a pre-season game and therefore not an official AFL game. In my first senior game I came on in the second half and absolutely killed it. Everything suddenly clicked. That feeling of being uncomfortable was gone. I felt like I belonged. I couldn't stop getting the ball, everywhere I went it followed, and I enjoyed every second of it.

In my first year I had felt myself improving and learning, and George had constantly encouraged me, but it was still difficult and I didn't feel comfortable myself. But that game changed everything. From that moment I had a whole different outlook and approach to training. My goal had gone from just wanting to play one AFL game at some point to wanting to play that one game in my second season, and as soon as possible. I became obsessed.

One of my main aims when I first arrived was to get the respect of the other players. I knew what they would be thinking: 'This Irish bloke is only over here to stuff around. He's got no idea and will never make it.' I hated that this might be what they were thinking, but I'd have thought the same if I'd seen an eighteen-year-old come to Ireland from another country and prance around like an idiot on a Gaelic pitch.

Gaining respect wasn't going to be easy, but I quickly figured the best place to earn it was on the training track. I identified very early on that Stuart Maxfield was the one to follow. He was one of the senior players and played on the wing, a position suited to fast, skilful players. As a young person I always looked around for someone older to model myself on, and Stewie was the one who stood out the most. At the start I didn't tell him that I was watching everything he did; instead, I just kept an eye on him at training. If he did 200 push-ups, I'd do 250. If he did two extra kicking sessions, I did three. It was one of the best things I did, because learning from and challenging myself against the best players was how I started to get better.

I was even giving blood for the cause, with my knuckles constantly bleeding because I was practising my handball so much. I found the best way to do it was to handball the football into a wall over and over again – a bit like I'd done with the Gaelic ball against the side of the family pub – and soon the skin on the knuckles of both hands was worn away. As a consequence I was forever putting plastic strips on my hands to try and stem the bleeding so I could get back to training.

One of the most valuable things Stewie taught me was how to read the game. In intra-club practice matches I would line up against him or Wayne Schwass, another of our experienced midfielders, and they would talk to me throughout the game about positioning. While my impulse was simply to chase after the ball, they taught me that the best way to get it was to predict where the ball was going to end up. Even though we were technically opponents in these games they would be in my ear saying, 'Wait. Hold back. Now go.' Learning on the job was the best way, and, thankfully, the skill of reading the game was something I managed to pick up quite quickly.

Aside from the training and playing side of things, another reason why things suddenly clicked into place for me was the fact that I was becoming more of an Aussie. What I mean is that I was finally coming to grips with the Australian culture, something that I'd struggled to grasp initially. Every day, even every hour, I would come across something that I'd never seen or even dreamed of before. My head was spinning almost every time I walked down the street.

The most pressing issue from the start was the food. Without a word of a lie, I ate spuds every day for eighteen years, yet at one of the first dinners I sat down to in Australia I was served asparagus. I had no idea what the hell these green sticks with pointy bits were (I actually love it now). Then there was the Aussie obsession with salads. Back home you always had a big feed of vegetables with your meat, and they were always hot. Not this cold mix of lettuce and fancy bean shoots and stuff thrown together. Bizarre.

And then there was Vegemite, an Australian tradition. Every person in the country eats it, either on their toast in the morning or whacked in the middle of a sandwich. I couldn't believe that this black shit, which tasted foul, was a national icon. Vegemite is to Australia what Guinness is to Ireland. That's how big it is. I absolutely hated it, which my teammates found quite amusing.

Adjusting to life in the very, very fast lane of Sydney naturally took a bit of getting used to. I mean, we're talking about going from a small Irish town of 4,000 to Australia's biggest and arguably most cosmopolitan city, with a population of over four million. Not that I saw much of it. For the first couple of years I didn't go into the city apart from at night to go to a nightclub. I stuck to the eastern suburbs, such as Coogee and, my absolute favourite, Bondi Beach. I had no interest in Sydney's famous landmarks, such as the Sydney Harbour Bridge and the Sydney Opera House, and it was only on the insistence of my parents, who enjoyed being tourists, that I did some sight-seeing.

The funny thing about me loving the Australian sun, sand and surf was the fact that I couldn't swim. This was a problem, given that most of our recovery from training and games involved going down to the pool or ocean for a swim. In the end Nathan Gibbs, the club's doctor, arranged for me to have lessons with his sister, who taught kids how to swim. So, I went down and was in the pool with these eight-year-olds, who just roared past me, absolutely blitzing me. I gradually got better, but only to the extent that I could maybe make it to one end of the pool. The hilarious thing was that I wasn't actually the worst swimmer at the Swans. Mickey O, who I had by now discovered to be one of funniest blokes I'd ever met, was easily the worst. We would often swim twenty-five metres and then stop and walk the rest. As for the ocean, I only went in as far as I could stand up – I never went out any deeper.

But I loved going to Bondi and would always say I was going for a recovery swim when really I was just lying on the beach and perving. I couldn't get over how many good-looking women there were in Sydney. I told all my mates back home that I'd landed in the greatest place in the world. My line when asked about my favourite stretch of beach was, 'I love Bondi. I love the scenery, and I'm not talking about the mountains and lakes.'

I found scenery of a very different kind in two of Sydney's more infamous haunts: Kings Cross and Oxford Street. The Cross is a seedy and very dodgy part of town, with numerous strip clubs and prostitutes lining every corner. It was an experience to go there at night, one that was better done in the safety of a car, with fellow giggling nineteen-year-olds who enjoyed cruising around the area and having chats with the ladies of the night.

Oxford Street was something completely different but just as shocking for a young lad from Ireland. While it was also a nightclub strip, it just happened to be the home of Sydney's gay community. I had never seen a gay person back home, so I'm sure you can imagine my reaction when I saw men walking around holding hands in these weird outfits. If that got my head spinning, it nearly exploded when I went to the world famous Sydney Gay & Lesbian Mardi Gras parade, which is held in Oxford Street every year in February. The street is closed to traffic for the night as thousands of gay people – they come from all over Australia and the world, with the event televised live on TV – dance on the back of floats in extraordinary costumes. I honestly thought I was on another planet the first time I saw it. It truly has to be seen to be believed.

Paul Kelly was the first one to give me the heads up about Oxford Street. One of landmarks of the area is a massive Coca-Cola sign, and Kel's invaluable advice when I first arrived was, 'If you ever see that big Coca-Cola sign and you are on your own, get the fuck out of there.'

Getting mobile was another big moment in my acclimatisation. Initially, I had caught lifts with teammates or, because I didn't want to feel like I was a hassle to anyone, I'd catch the bus, cycle or even run to training. In my second year I decided to go for my driving licence, but the law in Australia required you to be on 'L' plates for six months before you could apply for the full licence. Naturally, I did no practice until the morning of the test when I grabbed my teammate Stephen Doyle's car – he was a 7-foot ruckman who became one of my best mates – which was a big powerful six-cylinder

Mitsubishi Verada. I was then held up at training and arrived fifteen minutes late for the test. They had twenty-minute slots, so the tester wasn't happy.

She was even more cranky when I said, 'Sorry I'm late, but I got stuck in traffic.' I had driven to my test!

'You shouldn't have driven here,' she said, as it was illegal in Australia for a learner to drive on their own. I somehow talked my way around that one, and then I turned on the charm during the test. While I was driving I talked to the tester like she was my best friend, commenting on the weather and looking around as if I owned the road. My theory was that if you looked confident doing something, people would think that you were. I basically talked her into passing me, and I remember driving away thinking I was the biggest con artist.

Next on the agenda was a car. Being so wet behind the ears on so many levels, it's fair to say I didn't really look into the car-buying exercise too extensively. I simply walked into the bank, withdrew $7,000 in cash, put it in a backpack, walked out and caught a bus to the car yard. When I got there I put the backpack on the counter and said, 'Give me a car for seven grand.' It was just madness, but I was so naive that I figured that was what everyone did – turned up with backpacks full of cash to buy cars. If I'd asked the club for help, they probably could have arranged one for me or at least pointed me in the direction of a reputable dealer. In the end it all worked out, though, and I left a happy man in my new green Nissan Pulsar, which soon became known as 'Patsy the Pulsar'.

Me on my first birthday.

Me in the Sam Maguire cup, Gaelic football's ultimate prize.

Me and my brother Noel in our Sunday best.

Playing for my local club, the Listowel Emmets. That's me on the right with someone grabbing my jersey. Noel is on the ground pushing an opponent away from one of our players.

Me and Noel in Sydney on his first visit in 2003.

Me and Mum.

My Dad, 'the Horse', in action for Kerry in the Munster final against old rivals Cork, June 1982.

In my father's footsteps. Me in the Munster minor final 1999, also against the rebel county. I scored our only goal that day.

Knocked out. Me in the locker room, 20 September 2003, after losing the semi-final of the Premiership against the Brisbane Lions.

Hard work paying off. Getting away from Nathan Buckley to kick the winning goal against the Collingwood Magpies on 26 June 2004.

© Adam Pretty/Getty Images Sport/Getty Images

Representing my country in the International Rules Series was a huge honour. Here I am tangling with Adam McPhee at Croke Park on 17 October 2004.

CHAPTER 6

'I have never done this before.'

I was lying on the floor of the sitting room in Nathan Gibbs' house. He was standing over me with a pair of chopsticks in his hand. 'What?'

The reason the Sydney Swans' doctor was about to shove a chopstick up my nose was that it was actually pointing sideways. I had copped an elbow in my first game of the 2001 season with Port Melbourne, the team I was now playing for, as they had an alignment with the Swans. It was a great move by the club because each week seven players who were on the fringe of senior selection got the opportunity to travel to Melbourne to play in the Victorian Football League (VFL), which was a far superior standard to the local Sydney league.

However, my first taste of the new venture wasn't a very enjoyable one and continued a disturbing pattern when it came to injuries and first games. This time I was chasing after my opponent and lunged to grab him just as he was about to kick. As he did so his elbow swung back and nailed me right on the nose. The bone was smashed sideways, and when I got off the ground, with blood gushing everywhere, the Port

Melbourne doctor thought he should ring Gibbsy before he proceeded. He was ordered not to touch it and just send me back to Sydney immediately.

Gibbsy reckoned the chopstick was required to straighten the nose. I wasn't so sure, but before I could mount an argument he'd shoved it straight in. And when I say in, I'm talking so far up that it felt like it was in my forehead. Then he suddenly snapped it across, and I heard a crack that immediately forced me to jump up and start dry-retching. The sensation of the bone crunching back into position was the most painful thing I'd experienced in my life.

When the excruciating pain eventually subsided I managed to see the funny side and told Gibbsy and his wife Kerry that I'd be warning people about coming around to dinner parties at their house. 'I'll be saying, "If you ever go to Dr Gibbs' house, don't have Asian food, because he'll shove the chopsticks up your nose."'

A lot had changed in the previous twelve months. The same time the year before I had been crying myself to sleep because of homesickness; now I was playing in the VFL, and I had a manager and a girlfriend. The club had suggested that I should get someone to look after my affairs, as I was now pushing for senior selection and wouldn't be heading home at the end of my second year, as had been my original intention. A new contract would therefore need to be sorted out at some stage, so I spoke to one of my teammates, Amon Buchanan, who put me in touch with his manager, Michael Quinlan.

I had also managed to find myself a good Australian girl named Nicole. We went to university together, and she had also been a barmaid at The Palace, one of the nightclubs in Coogee that the boys liked to frequent. I was surprised we'd actually got past our first date – it was when I didn't have a car, so my flatmate Crouchy had to drive me to her house to pick her up and then onto the restaurant. Nicole seemed a bit bemused, and dinner wasn't much better. We went to a fancy place called The Blue Room near Fox Studios, and I ordered a dish that had a vegetable in it that I later found out was called pak choi. I had no idea what I was eating, but as I was trying to impress I picked up this green shit and pretended to enjoy every mouthful. Nicole didn't say much for the entire date, so I didn't think there would be another, but I'd obviously done enough to get a second chance.

My rapid improvement following my pre-season breakthrough saw me elevated from the rookie list in round two and named as an emergency for the senior team. (Emergencies are listed in case there is an injury before the game starts and they can come in as a replacement, but once the game starts they play no part.) Finally, I felt like my goal was within reach. However, it remained at arms' length for quite a while, as my name became a seemingly permanent fixture on the emergency list. The fourth time I was named there I got a phone call from Rocket just as I landed in Melbourne on a Friday night. He wanted me to turn around and get back on the plane to Sydney because something had happened to Stuart Maxfield, and there was a doubt as to whether he would be fit for the Swans game against Melbourne club the Western Bulldogs.

As soon as I got off the phone, I rang my manager. 'It looks like I'm playing my first senior game,' I said to Michael. 'Apparently, Stewie Maxfield is not fit.'

They were going to give him until the morning to see if he recovered from his niggling injury. I didn't get much sleep that night and I was psyched when I arrived at the ground, but my excitement was short-lived, as Stewie had been declared fit to play. So, instead of making my AFL debut, I was forced to play in the local league, because I couldn't get back down to Port Melbourne in time. I played terribly. The standard was shit, which is exactly how I played, setting back my senior prospects for a couple of weeks.

During this time, George was continually in Rocket's ear, because the senior team was going through a rough trot. 'Rocket, you've got to play him,' he kept saying. 'We need a run. You've got to play him.'

Rocket wasn't convinced and his standard reply was, 'I'm not playing the Irishman.'

Finally, after being on the emergency list seven times in the first half of the season, I got the phone call I'd been dreaming about, in the lead-up to the round fourteen clash at the SCG against Carlton.

It was a Thursday lunchtime when Rocket rang and said the magical words, 'You're in.' A second after I got off the phone from the coach I rang Ireland to tell Mum and Dad, even though it was four in the morning. They were thrilled, and I thought it would be great if they could make it out, but Dad had been sick. Also, the game was that Sunday, so it wasn't very realistic.

I couldn't have wished for a better birthday present – I'd turned twenty the previous Sunday – and I was the toast of Sydney when I arrived at training the next day. There was press everywhere, and suddenly I had become 'Mr Media Man', which was a bit overwhelming. They could see how excited I was, and I said, 'I could die a happy man on Monday.'

I was jumping out of my skin at training, and I was a bit worried that I was so nervous now, as I could only imagine what I'd be like on Sunday. Once I got a few touches of the ball I started to feel better and managed to calm myself down. We had a team meeting after training in which we talked about the line-up, how the opposition might set up and our own tactics. Rocket told me to focus on simply enjoying the occasion. I understood what he meant, but putting it into practice wasn't going to be very easy.

I had the rest of Friday and Saturday off, so I figured I would wrap myself in cotton wool and not leave the house in case I got hurt. I made one exception – a visit to the video store. I figured that watching movies would be a good way for my mind to stay busy and not think about the game. However, keeping my excitement level under control went out the window when I got a phone call from Phil Mullen. 'Your Mum is on her way over,' he said. 'She'll be in Sydney at 6 a.m. on the morning of the game.'

I was shocked. And to use an Aussie saying I had picked up, I was pumped. It turned out Dad's illness – a heart problem – had forced him into hospital, so he obviously couldn't make the trip. That was disappointing, but at least Mum, the person who had initially been so against me coming to Australia, would be there to witness my big moment.

My plans for an easy Saturday didn't come together, as I must have talked to the whole town of Listowel and used every piece of available technology. I was talking on the phone, sending text messages or emailing. It was great to hear from everyone and the support I received was unbelievable, but it was all too much, and I wasn't able to relax. My hopes of a good night's sleep didn't happen, and I tossed and turned all night before waking up at 7 a.m. bleary eyed. I must have had only about one hour of sleep. I went to mass at the local church to get some divine inspiration, and when I got home Mum arrived on my doorstep.

It was so good to see her, and she immediately put me at ease. We had breakfast together and I was so enjoying talking about everything back at home that for the first time in four days I wasn't thinking about my senior debut. Mum left for the match at 11 a.m., and I got a lift soon after with Crouchy to the ground. We watched a bit of the reserves game before going inside for a meeting. I was starting on the bench, which was good, because it would give me time to take everything in and try to calm down.

With an hour until kick-off, I got my ankles strapped and then had a massage from one of the trainers for twenty minutes. I then meticulously put on my boots and my number forty-one jumper before joining my teammates on the ground for the pre-game warm-up. A few of the boys were offering me advice. Mickey O and Andrew Dunkley, one of our experienced defenders, just told me to get it and kick it, which was fine by me. There was a lot of tension in the build-up, and the players' focus was unbelievable. We'd lost our last three games, so this match against second-placed Carlton was vital for our season, and I could sense the urgency of the situation. I was fully switched on. I only broke my concentration momentarily to give Mum a kiss just before we headed onto the field.

As I ran out, I looked around and was delighted to see some Irish flags in the crowd, but I was absolutely shitting myself. After a few run-throughs I was extremely happy to be going to the bench, because I needed to pull myself together. I was thinking I'd probably sit out the first quarter and maybe get more of a run in the second half when the pace of the game might have slowed down a bit. When the siren sounded I was still in my own little world and had slipped into spectator mode when I heard someone call out my name from the other end of the bench. 'Tadhg, you're going on.'

What the?

Wayne Schwass was running towards the boundary line. He'd done something wrong, and Rocket was pulling him off so that he could let him know from the coach's box exactly what with one of his famous verbal sprays which left you in no doubt about his thoughts on the situation. I stood up, flung off my jacket and walked over to the interchange gate. As I ran on there was a massive roar from the crowd. It literally sent a shiver down my spine, and I had 100 things going through my mind.

What do I do? Am I ready for this? Where do I stand? What if the ball comes over here?

I was only on for thirty seconds, but it struck me how hot it was out on the field. Maybe it was a combination of my nerves and the unusually warm winter's day, but it certainly affected me. The good thing about my short burst was that I at least knew what to expect next time, and it got a lot of adrenalin out of my system. I didn't go on again until five minutes into the second quarter, and I pretty much stayed on for the rest of the game. I picked up a few possessions on the wing and managed to stay calm, which was what I had repeatedly been telling myself to do during the build-up.

The game was going down to the wire, and I was back on the bench with fifteen minutes to go when I was handed the phone, as Rocket wanted a chat. 'I want you to run everywhere with Craig Bradley,' he said. 'I don't want him to touch the fucking ball.'

Bradley was one of Carlton's superstars. I went back on and locked myself onto him. I didn't care where the ball was or what was happening around me; wherever Bradley went, I was all over him. I actually lost track of the score, which had been close all day, but when the siren sounded I realised we'd done it. Sydney had won by ten points. I couldn't believe we'd pulled it off, and one of the first people to jump on me was George Stone. He sprinted onto the ground – something he later told me he'd never done before in his life – and wrapped me up in the biggest bear hug. We had been through so much, having basically spent nearly every day of the previous couple of years together, working towards this moment. I had finished my first AFL game with seven kicks, one handball, three marks and one tackle.

It was mayhem in the changing-room afterwards as we sang the club's theme song with some serious passion. Mum came down, and I saw her wipe a tear from her eye. I felt myself well up too. There was a function after the match that we went to, and then on the ride home I finally got the chance to be alone with her. She told me how excited everyone around her had been when I ran onto the ground. As I listened to her describe a day she would never forget I had an overwhelming urge to cry again. I had shed plenty of tears in Australia over the previous eighteen months, but these were tears of joy, because I knew this was only the beginning.

A few days later I got a phone call that topped off an extraordinary week. It was from the Irish International Rules team manager Brian McEniff, informing me that I'd been selected to join the Ireland squad for the next series, which was to be played in Australia in October 2001.

I managed to hold my spot on the senior team for the next three weeks as we got on a roll, winning all our games to put us in the frame for the finals. However, after having only three touches against the Perth-based West Coast Eagles, in round seventeen, I was sent back to Port Melbourne for a couple of weeks to find form. I was brought back for the round twenty game against Melbourne at the SCG and responded by producing my best performance so far, grabbing fifteen possessions and kicking my first goal in AFL football. It was a great moment. I ran past Mickey O, who gathered the ball in the forward pocket and hit me with a quick handball. There was no one in front of me, and the goals were just twenty metres away, so I steadied and tried to do the best drop-punt I could. It came off the boot perfectly and split the middle of the goalposts. I raised both arms in the air to celebrate before being converged on by my teammates.

We then travelled to Brisbane for the final game of the home-and-away season, and I played myself into a spot for the finals by kicking two goals. Unfortunately, my debut in the finals wasn't a fairy tale like my senior debut. We played Melbourne club the Hawthorn Hawks in an elimination final at Colonial Stadium (now Docklands Stadium), an incredible indoor stadium in Melbourne with a retractable roof, although the playing surface was a major disappointment. I found myself playing most of the match because two of our players, Ryan O'Keefe and Dale Lewis, were taken off with serious injuries inside the first ten minutes. We hung in there and were leading at half-time, but they smashed us in the second half, kicking fourteen goals to four.

Rocket was fuming afterwards but managed to give me a compliment by default when he was giving ruckman Greg Stafford a spray for a bad kicking error he'd made. 'This fucking Irish kid still doesn't know how to kick the ball, and he was one of our best players,' Rocket said.

While I pretended to be sombre like everyone else, inside I was very excited. My first season of AFL football had been a massive success for me. I had set out to play one game and had ended up playing eight, including one in the finals, when the coach had described me as one of the team's best players. Now my attitude was, 'Bring on next year.'

But first I had some business to attend to with my own country. It was a great honour to wear the Ireland jersey in the International Rules series, which we won 2–0. It was funny playing against a couple of my Sydney teammates, Stewie Maxfield and Adam Goodes, and I thrived in the games because I was the best suited of anyone to the hybrid game. I ticked every box. I'd lived in Ireland and played Gaelic football, and I'd also lived in Australia and played Aussie rules. I played particularly well in the second test match at the MCG, which caused a bit of a stir back home. The game was telecast back in Ireland, and one of the analysts, former Meath All-Ireland star Colm O'Rourke, said the Kerry Group, who were Kerry's major sponsor, needed to dig into their pockets and 'get this kid home real quick'. The following year, they nearly did.

GEORGE STONE

'In my opinion it's one of the great sporting stories, to see someone come from the other side of the world, not play the game, not grow up with the game, and then make such a great fist of it. I'm talking about the impact he had, playing in a Premiership-winning side, being in the Swans' leadership group, it really is an amazing sporting story.

'It was hard enough for me to develop kids who had been playing all their life, let alone a skinny Irish kid who had just turned eighteen and didn't know anything about footy. Kicking was the key. If he was going to make it, he had to be able to kick. Rocket was of the opinion that if you couldn't kick, you couldn't play. That applied to the whole list, so I knew if Tadhg was going to get anywhere, he had to be able to kick.

'We started with a blank canvas. We used to stand him on the fence so he had to kick straight through, straight down the line of the fence, which stopped him from kicking around the corner, like they did in Gaelic football.

'It was obvious to me early on that he was going to give it a real crack, and that was a real bonus. If he was willing to do all the work, there was a chance, because he was a talent, he could run, he had ball skills and he knew where the ball was going. It was just a matter of getting the kicking right, and that's what we spent a lot of time on. He knew that if you couldn't hit a target at training, it didn't matter who you were, Rocket would give you a spray. He knew that to keep in Rocket's good books he had to get his kicking right.

'He had to learn a lot of things, and there were times when it wasn't fun. It was pretty frustrating, and that's when he made the statement that he only wanted to play one game. He didn't want to play 100; he just wanted to play one game. When it clicked for him in 2001, I was on Rocket's case about playing him. Initially he couldn't get his head around selecting an Irishman, but I eventually wore him down, and Tadhg got picked for the game against Carlton at the SCG. After the game, which we won, I did something that I'd never done before: I was so excited that I ran onto the ground and jumped on him. It took me back to when we first started and how his aim was to play just one game and he'd done it.

'Homesickness was always an issue, but I can't say how an Australian kid would fare in Ireland. I mean, look at AFL star Chris Judd: he wanted to come home to Victoria from Western Australia. Here we are talking about a kid from a completely different culture. I was always nervous when he went home at Christmas.

'I remember we were going over to Ireland to do another clinic, and we got Tadhg to do a video message for the Irish kids about what it was like to play with the Sydney Swans. At the end of it we asked him, "What else do you like about Australia, Tadhg?"

'He stared down the barrel of the camera and said, "I love the girls. There are lots of girls about, so come out here, boys, because there are plenty of girls." We ended up having to cut it, but that was typical Tadhg.

'He really became an incredible player. I mean, in the 2005 Grand Final he ran down the wing and kicked a goal. I was amazed that he'd become such a valuable player, someone the opposition were trying to stop every week. He even started to kick in from full-back and that shows how good a kicker he became, because that is not a simple exercise. You have the pressure of pin-pointing a teammate after a behind is scored while the entire focus of every one at the ground is on you. You have to hit your targets or else the ball is going to come back over your head for a goal.

'I went over to Listowel for Tim's funeral and was blown away by what a legend he was in Kerry. There were photos of him everywhere, and it gave me an understanding of how the county would have been horrified that the son of a great Kerry player had turned his back on Gaelic footy and travelled to the other side of the world. It was a really moving experience, and the funeral had a big impact on me in a lot of ways.

'When I came back I thought it would have an even bigger impact on Tadhg. I said to the Swans that he would return to Ireland. For the first three years he was here I always told him to keep going, keep chipping away at the AFL, because he was still young enough to go back and play Gaelic footy, but after the Premiership and after the death of his father it was going to be harder and harder to keep him in Australia.

'He had tremendous strength of mind, but he played when

he shouldn't have and that contributed to him going home eventually, because with the injuries he was getting he figured if he kept playing here, he wouldn't be able to go back and play over there.

'What he did is an amazing achievement, and I don't think he'll stop at that. I actually said to him that I think he might be prime minister of Ireland one day, and that would be good because then he can pull a few strings for me when I come over to visit.'

CHAPTER 7

My phone beeped, and I saw it was another call from Ireland. Almost every day someone from the homeland would give me a shout. Usually it was one of my extended family who was up for a chat. This time it was someone completely different and unexpected. Jack O'Connor, the manager of Kerry's Under-21 team, was on the line and wanted to know when I was coming home.

I'd just completed my second season as a senior player in the AFL, and it had been a disappointing one for the Swans. We didn't make the finals, which meant I would be back in Ireland at the start of September 2002. Jack was happy about that, because I would be back in time for the All-Ireland semi-finals. 'Well, I would like you to come in and train, and we'll see how you get on,' O'Connor said.

It was a great opportunity, because I still had plans to go back and play Gaelic football again. There was no problem stepping back in, as I knew most of the players, and the game itself was like riding a bike: you never forget. I did enough in training to get picked on the panel for the semi-final and came on fairly early into the match as a substitute. From the moment I stepped on it was like I was thrown back five years. I was a teenager again, running around without a care in the world. It showed in my performance, and I played really well. Unfortunately, it wasn't enough, and we lost the game.

However, it was enough for me to get another unexpected phone call, this time from the Kerry senior manager, Páidí Ó Sé. He had played alongside my father in the Kerry golden era and had won an extraordinary eight All-Irelands with the Kingdom. 'Do you want to come to training and give us a hand?' Ó Sé asked.

Noel was part of the senior team, although he was currently sidelined because of a groin problem. Kerry had already won through to the All-Ireland final, so I was just there to train with the guys for three weeks, throw myself around and offer them something different. That was my initial intention, but things started to change a bit as my form started to show out on the track, and the rumour mill then went into overdrive after I dominated an inter-club trial game. People started talking about me, and suddenly I was a hot topic of conversation leading up to the All-Ireland final. Everyone was asking, 'Will he or won't he play?' The problem was I started listening.

People inside the camp told me that I would be on the panel, and one of the assistant coaches virtually gave me the nod the day before the side was to be announced. Noel had watched all the training, and he thought I'd be selected. I couldn't believe I had a chance to play in a Senior All-Ireland final, something I had dreamed about all my life.

The panel was being named on Tuesday night, and I found myself staring at the phone waiting for the call. When it came it wasn't what I was expecting. 'We're not going with you,' Páidí said.

I couldn't believe it. I had built myself up so much, got my hopes up so high, and all for nothing. When I hung up the phone I was seriously pissed off, as much with myself as Páidí. I knew I shouldn't have got caught up in all the talk, but they'd asked me to train and had instigated the whole thing. The bottom line was that I and everyone else knew that I was good enough to be on that team. That was a fact I struggled to deal with over the next few days.

I watched the final in the crowd with my father. The whole episode had been hard on him, as he and Páidí were the best of best friends. They'd been close on the field – Dad played centre-back and Páidí right half-back – with the bond even stronger off the field, and they were constant drinking buddies. Dad didn't want to get involved, but I think he understood where his good friend was coming from. It was hard to leave out someone who had trained and played all year in favour of me.

Kerry were playing Armagh in the final. At half-time the game seemed over, with Kerry dominating, leading by four points and kicking with the wind in the second half. However, Armagh scored a goal out of nowhere at the fifty-fifth minute, and suddenly Kerry were in trouble. For the final seventeen minutes Kerry failed to score, and Armagh took an unlikely victory by a point.

I became quite emotional after the final whistle and was actually close to tears as I left Croke Park. The situation wasn't helped by the number of Kerry fans who came up to me and said, 'We would have won it if you'd been playing, Tadhg.'

Three weeks later I was rooming with Armagh captain Kieran McGeeney during the International Rules series, which was being held in Ireland. He told me that he'd been shitting himself that I would come out after half-time and line up at centre half-forward against him. Hearing that made me feel even worse.

Slowly, as time went by, I came to the realisation that not playing was actually the best thing. If I had played and won an All-Ireland medal that way, I probably wouldn't have appreciated it as much as if I'd worked all year to do it. I came to the conclusion that it just wouldn't have been right.

I heard later that Páidí had spoken to his former coach Mick O'Dwyer, a man regarded as one of the greatest managers in the history of the sport, having guided Kerry to ten All-Ireland finals, winning eight of them. He had rung O'Dwyer on the Monday, the day before he had to make the decision, and asked whether he should play me. 'When I was a manager, I always went with my gut,' O'Dwyer told him.

When I eventually spoke about it with Páidí he admitted he'd ignored the advice of his teacher. 'I didn't go with my gut,' he said. 'I went with my head, thinking I shouldn't do it.'

The Kerry experience topped off what had been a funny sort of a year. My obsession with playing AFL had gone up a level following on from my debut season. In the lead-up to the 2002 season I had trained like never before. I had moved into a new house with my giant mate Doyley – he was a 6 foot 8 inches and 105 kilogram ruckman – and Scott Stevens in Botany, which was just next door to Bondi. The house was owned by Rowan Warfe, another Sydney player, and the previous tenants had been three of our teammates: Ryan Fitzgerald, Heath James and Jude Bolton. So you can imagine the state of the house when we arrived. It wasn't about to improve in a hurry either, as we used to play all sorts of games inside, including cricket, a sport which Australians were fascinated by but one I struggled to get my head around. Despite this, I was as competitive as anyone during our games in the hallway, in which we used the shaft of a golf club as the bat.

The three of us became as thick as thieves, and it was a perfect set-up for the club's dietitian, as we were all skinny beanpoles who desperately needed to put on weight. Being in the one house meant we could push each other to try and stack on some size, as it had been made clear to us that we needed to if we wanted to become AFL senior players. The club taught us how to cook, and for the first time in my life I was introduced to pasta – as I've said, my carbohydrate fix at home had been spuds, spuds and more spuds. We would cook up massive pots of pasta, usually accompanied by a bolognese sauce, and have enormous portions. One night Doyley broke the record, taking three hours to complete his meal. It was hilarious watching him have a go at it, then have to go away for a rest and then come back and go at it again. The Swans just wanted us to eat and eat and eat. We'd eat bowls of cereal half an hour before dinner just to help put on weight – we were really eating like animals. We'd also have protein shakes every few hours, because we were doing so much training that we'd burn off most of the food.

Eventually though, the club became concerned that I was eating too many carbohydrates and that my milk drinking was way over the top. I was a big, big milk drinker. I always had been. If I was thirsty, I could slug down a litre of milk in a heartbeat. The Aussies thought I was weird, because when they were thirsty they had cordial or water, definitely not milk.

Everything we did was about putting on size and developing ourselves as footballers. Every morning we would get up and do 50 to 100 push-ups together. It was a house rule, and it didn't matter if you had a later start than the other two – you were still required to get out of bed and do the push-ups. You could then go back to bed if you wanted. We also regularly got up early before training, sometimes at 6 a.m., and went to the park, which was just down the street, with a handball target to practise our skills. We'd do hundreds of handballs each, then go back home, grab some breakfast and head to training. It was full on, but we knew it was the only way to fast-track our careers.

I was so skinny when I first got to Sydney that I often joked that I put on weight just by walking through the door of the gym. The difference in mindsets between Australia and Ireland when it came to putting on weight was significant. Back home the mindset was that if you put on too much weight, it would slow you down. That was a complete myth, because increasing muscle weight actually makes you go quicker. I mean, look at those 100-metre sprinters at the Olympics. They are monsters and get power from their muscle mass.

It probably took me more than a year to put on ten kilograms. I'd never lifted a bar in my life before George took me into the weights room. He had to show me everything – the proper technique to lift and how much to put on where. The boys were pissing themselves as they watched me struggle to lift forty kilograms on the bench press. 'That's it, Tadhg,' they'd say. 'Do you want us to put another CD on there for you?'

I started the year where I'd left off, in the senior team, and held my spot for the first eight rounds until I was dropped for the biggest game of the season, against Melbourne club Essendon. Everyone had been looking forward to it, because it was the first AFL game to be played at the Olympic Stadium in Homebush. Doyley was also dropped for the game, and we found out on the Thursday-night training session, which was held at the new stadium. We were both really pissed off and drove home at 100 miles per hour, behaving like lunatics, doing these crazy handbrake skids.

When we got home Doyley said he was going to bed, which enraged me even more, and in typical Irish tradition I said, 'Fuck this. There is no way I'm going to bed. I'm going on the piss.'

Sydney has a very large Irish community, so I was always running into fellow countrymen. I had actually kept away from that world during my first two years while I tried to get my career started, but every now and then I would slip into it, and this was one of those occasions. I rang up an Irish guy I'd met a few months earlier and went for a few pints. A few turned into a lot and I woke up the next morning with a massive hangover.

I was still feeling sick when we flew down to Melbourne that afternoon, with Port Melbourne playing the next day. Doyley was laughing at how sick I was, but I was the one doing the laughing the following day. Despite my unusual preparation, I was best-on-ground in the VFL game, while my ruckman had a shocker. I got straight back into the seniors the following week and never looked back.

The Swans weren't a very enjoyable team to play for for much of that season, with the players and coach at loggerheads. Morale was down, and we'd fallen into a serious midseason slump, losing five games in a row. After the fifth loss against Geelong at home in round twelve, the players got together and hit the town. Some bonding was desperately needed, but we paid for it the next morning when we arrived for our normal recovery session to find a less than happy Rocket waiting for us. Instead of a leisurely swim or some treadmill action, he ordered a brutal weights session. The next day he resigned.

Although I'd been scared of him for most of my time at the club Rocket had taught me a lot about the game, particularly tactics and reading the play. He was the one who had given me my opportunity, and for that I would forever be indebted to him. Paul Roos, Rocket's assistant, took over in a caretaker role. He'd been a legendary player in the AFL with both Fitzroy, a club that no longer existed, and Sydney. He had played a remarkable 356 games, mainly at centre half-back, and had only retired in 1998. For the players it was certainly a case of going from one extreme to the other, with Roosy an absolute favourite amongst the boys. That was obvious in the way we played for him, starting with a victory in his first game, against Fremantle. There was a drastic change in the game plan, with the players basically told just to go out and play. The shackles were released by our new coach for the final ten games of the season and they were easily the most enjoyable I had played.

There had been a lot of fear playing under Rocket, especially for young players. You felt that if you made a mistake, you'd be dropped the next week, or if you made an error, at quarter-time or half-time the coach would blow the shit out of you. The fear had always been there, both at training and in the games. It was unhealthy and forced a lot of players to go into their shells and not express themselves.

Word got out near the end of the year that Western Bulldogs coach Terry Wallace was set to walk, as he had been guaranteed the Sydney job by the club's board. The Sydney players didn't want a bit of this, and in the final game of the season, against Melbourne team Richmond at Telstra Stadium, we made a statement. I was actually in doubt before the game because of a bad case of the flu, but I was desperate to be there so played off the interchange bench for most of the night. I spent more time than usual coming on and off the bench that night, because I wasn't a hundred per cent. When the siren sounded on another win – we had won six of our last ten games under our new coach – the players gathered in the middle of the ground and lifted Roosy onto our shoulders. It was a real defining moment. We were telling the board that this was our man, and the Sydney crowd got behind us. Thankfully, people power won in the end, and Roos was given the job, with the Swans board forced to back away from the rumoured arrangement with Wallace, who'd made an inglorious exit from the Bulldogs. Appointing Roos would prove to be an inspired move.

Chapter 8

The Irish experiment. That was what I was called during my first few years in Sydney, and it drove me nuts. I hated the expression, as it sounded like I had come from a test tube in a laboratory. The problem was that it was repeated over and over again in the media when they were referring to my development as a player. It was frustrating because I wasn't an experiment. My aim was to become a big-time player.

Roosy had his own experiment planned for me. I'd played most of my football so far on the wing or at half-forward, but he had visions of playing me at half-back. Life as a defender didn't really appeal to me, as I always saw myself as a forward scoring and setting up goals. Roosy's selling point was that I had a licence to run and create as much as I wanted, and it only took me a couple of pre-season games to realise the new senior coach had found me my niche in AFL football.

The pre-season had been particularly enjoyable because Noel had come over in February for six weeks. He'd had constant groin and hernia problems the previous year, and I asked him to send his scans over so that Gibbsy could have a look at them. I knew a couple of our players, including Adam Goodes, had suffered the same problem and had been successfully operated on in Sydney. Gibbsy took one look at Noel's scans and booked him in for surgery.

It was great having him stay with me and just reinforced that it should have happened on a permanent basis years earlier. One of my biggest regrets was not asking the club to have a look at Noel when I first came over. He had clearly been the best minor in Ireland when he was seventeen, and if the Swans had been looking then, he would have definitely been the one selected. The problem was that by the time I came over in 1999 he was already an established player in the Kerry senior team. And when I had my debut in 2001 he had already won a senior All-Ireland medal, so his GAA career had really gone that level too far. In hindsight I should have been stronger about it, but I suppose back then I was more worried about my own survival.

After a shaky start to the 2003 season we got our act together under our new coach and won eleven out of thirteen matches between rounds five and seventeen, to put ourselves in the Premiership race. The turnaround had been spectacular under Roosy, and the winning habit was something I was getting used to.

I was very much a creature of habit when it came to preparation for games. Some people would have said I was a bit of a freak, which was probably fair enough when I look back on my meticulous pre-game antics. My belief was that if something worked, and by that I mean I played a good game, then the exact same preparation would be followed the next week. Every single thing was identical: what time I ate, what I ate, where I ate, who I talked to. But if I had a shocker, it all went out the window and I would change everything.

A typical game day would generally start with a big breakfast of cereal, toast, yoghurt, muesli, fruit and scrambled eggs, with a couple of bottles of Powerade to hydrate. Then it was off to the local Catholic church in Botany, because I found it helped bring me down to earth. After that a quick game of *Grand Turismo* on the PlayStation would keep my mind occupied before I really started to click into game mode by writing down a list of goals, which I packed in my bag and referred to in the car on the way to the ground and then again before I ran out.

Before I left home, I liked to run hot water on my lower back in the shower and eat a honey sandwich. In my kit bag was the same ankle sock I'd had since my first game, which I wore on my right kicking foot. I'd been wearing two socks on my kicking foot since I was junior back in Ireland because it made it feel tighter in the boot and more comfortable. I had worn the same blue underpants in every AFL game, and they had deteriorated to the point that I had to tape them to my skin. Plus, I had worn the same pair of red shorts since I'd been at the Swans, and I always had the tag of my shorts hanging out, which also stemmed from my junior days. I used to do it because I knew it pissed my mother off and had just continued with it. I also liked to have my jumper tucked into my shorts and be the last one to run onto the field. The problem was that there were a couple of other players who had the same superstition. It became a running joke with Andrew Schauble and Ben Matthews, as we'd be fighting each other to see who would be last. Those two used to try and sabotage my routine by sticking my tag back into my shorts as we were about to run out.

A perfect example of my superstitious ways was when I broke my hand playing cricket in our house. I was doing my best Shane Warne impersonation and came in to bowl a leg-spinner, but, unfortunately, I smashed my hand down on the top of the couch on my follow through. I immediately stuck my finger in a some ice, thinking it wasn't anything serious, but when I was at the beach later it was still killing me, so I decided to ring Gibbsy, as we had a big game the following day. When I was driving over to see him I couldn't squeeze the steering wheel, which made me think I was in a bit of trouble. He had a look at it and said he'd give me a small amount of painkiller. If it worked, I would be able to play and he wouldn't tell anyone. If it didn't work, he would have to ring Roosy straight away. I knew that if it didn't work, I'd still say it was fine, because there was no way a stupid little broken finger was going to keep me out. I decided to wear a glove to protect the finger and proceeded to play one of my best games, earning three Brownlow Medal votes from the umpires for my performance. I kept wearing the glove from then on, even when my hand came good, and to this day Roosy still doesn't know anything about the cricket incident.

Funnily enough, I wasn't hung up about what number I wore, as a lot of players were, because in Gaelic football numbers weren't important. However, after two years of wearing number forty-one I did trade it in for a lower, more respectable number. I was given number seventeen, which was perfect given that my birthday was the first of the seventh month and, of course, St Patrick's Day was 17 March.

A major factor in why we'd become a very good side was the recruitment of Barry Hall from St Kilda, who'd had his troubles down in Melbourne, both on and off the field. Historically, the Swans had a great history of taking on troubled souls and straightening them out. Tony Lockett, or 'Plugger' as he was known, was the greatest success story. He also came from St Kilda and flourished in the Harbour City, taking the Swans to a Grand Final in 1996 and breaking the AFL goalkicking record. The change of scenery worked wonders for Tony and Barry, as they could go about their business as relative unknowns in Sydney, whereas down in Melbourne their every move was scrutinised. Plugger retired in 1999 but was lured back to playing in 2002. The big man, who stood at 6 foot 3 inches and 104 kilograms, only lasted three games, adding three goals to his record haul, which finished at 1,360 goals.

When I first arrived I had no idea who any of these legends were, and in a way I think it helped me on the training track because I wasn't in awe of someone like Plugger or Paul Kelly. If we were doing a competitive drill, I'd be going at them just like anyone else. I think that helped me win over their respect, whereas other youngsters who had grown up admiring these players might have felt overwhelmed in their presence. I didn't care because I simply didn't know.

Like Plugger, Hally was a key forward and a scary individual. There weren't many meaner-looking lads on a football field than him, and he had a short fuse and a quick right jab to go with it. He was certainly an intimidating force, and in our first final against Port Adelaide in Adelaide Hally made the difference. He kicked six goals as we pulled off a massive upset to progress through to the preliminary final. Port had finished on top at the end of the home-and-away season, but we dominated the game in the first half and led by forty points at half-time. They came back hard at us, but we held on to win by two goals. I was so thankful we did because victory meant we got a week off, and I needed all of that time to get over the worst corkie (dead leg) I'd ever experienced, courtesy of a tackle by Port's tough man Damien Hardwick.

The frustrating thing was I'd had a really good first half. Roosy had started me at forward in a bit of shock tactic in the first quarter which paid off and then I went back to half-back and found plenty of ball. But at the five-minute mark of the third quarter, Hardwick just ran straight through me and severely corked my quad in the process. It felt like my leg was dead. After he'd done it, he stood over me while I was on the ground and started laughing. I wanted to throttle the bastard, but I couldn't move. I had to be helped off the ground, and I was still on crutches that night because I couldn't walk. There was no way I could have played the following week if we'd been required to.

We came up against Brisbane in the preliminary final, which was played on our home turf at Telstra Stadium. The Lions had won the past two Premierships and were on target to become one of the greatest teams of all time. After a week of icing my leg it had finally come good, and we were confident that a Grand Final berth was ours for the taking, with the consensus being that the Lions dynasty was on its last legs. That was what we were screaming to each other at the three-quarter-time huddle, as we'd just kicked four goals to two and were now just three points behind.

The next thirty minutes were a disaster. Instead of Brisbane falling apart, we did. We only scored one point in the final quarter and were humiliated by forty-four points. The ending didn't do the season justice, with Roosy's first year as coach a stunning success, given that we had gone from eleventh to playing in a preliminary final. I had played every game – chalking up my fiftieth in round twenty-two – and was starting to feel comfortable and confident around the place. My knowledge of the game had improved dramatically, and I was definitely coming out of my shell and expressing myself more on the field as a leader. I was starting to become a player.

As the sun beat down and the sweat started to form under my suit I was cursing whoever had put me up to this. I was sitting outside the Sydney Opera House, looking up at the Sydney Harbour Bridge, surrounded by media and TV cameras, waiting to receive my Australian citizenship. While that in itself was crazy, the most disturbing fact was that they'd scheduled the big PR stunt the day after the city's St Patrick's Day celebrations. Seriously, what were they thinking?

As a result I was in a world of pain. Next to me my manager Michael looked to be in a similar state, as he'd come up from Melbourne the night before and had indulged in some of the festivities to celebrate Ireland's biggest day. The whole idea of the Australian citizenship had been cooked up by the government and the football club. They needed someone to promote the national launch of 'Harmony Day', which, according to the press release I'd been shown, was a federal government initiative to build the cohesiveness of Australia's multicultural society and tackle issues of prejudice and racism. I'm not sure why they thought I was the man to bring the world together, but the AFL were heavily involved in the event, which was the reason I was front and centre, trying my hardest not to keel over.

The first thing I'd actually thought of when I'd been approached was that it would be a lot easier to get through customs with an Australian passport. No more waiting in the non-Australian line; I would be fast-tracked through. That was all I thought about, because while I might have been getting duel citizenship I never considered myself Australian. I was an Irishman through and through, but the passport would certainly come in handy.

We had taken a bus from the SCG to the ceremony. All the bigwigs were involved, with the Swans' chief executive Myles Baron-Hay on board along with Roosy and players Andrew Schauble, Mickey O and Goodesy. My girlfriend Nicole was also there for moral support.

As part of the ceremony, I was required to stand up and sing the national anthem. I think we'd been expected to learn it beforehand, but I only knew a few lines. Unfortunately, the cameras were aimed straight at me, so I put my head down and mumbled something for the lines I didn't know, and when it hit the chorus up I came and bellowed out 'Advance Australia Fair'. Then I put my head down again. I think I did enough to bluff my way through. On the odd occasion when the national anthem was played before games, I would actually sing the Irish national anthem, which is in Gaelic. My teammate Adam Schneider, who was as superstitious as I was, would always make sure he was standing next to me, and he enjoyed my foreign twist to what was supposed to be a serious moment.

The next pressing issue was handling the presentation. I was called up to receive my certificate from the Minister for Citizenship and Multicultural Affairs, the Honourable Gary Hardgrave. I shook his hand, posed for a photo and then decided to sit down again immediately. I think they were expecting me to make a big speech, declaring my love for Australia and how I was an Aussie at heart, but I was concerned about stringing a coherent sentence together, as my resistance to my hangover had started to fail.

I then posed for more photos, as they wanted some with me and Nicole and the bridge in the background. I still managed to drop a joke for the journalists. 'Sorry, darl,' I said to Nicole, 'but now I've got this [citizenship], I don't need you any more.'

Things were a little bit more serious a couple of weeks later as the countdown to round one of the 2004 season was heating up. We were up against Brisbane, who had gone on after defeating us in the preliminary final to blow Collingwood away in the Grand Final and win their third consecutive Premiership, at the Gabba Stadium in Queensland. It was a massive opening game of the season, and tensions were high during our main training session on the Wednesday. In fact, we hadn't trained very well, which moved Stewie Maxfield, who had replaced Paul Kelly as captain the previous year, to call us in and deliver a good old-fashioned spray. 'This is fucking shit,' he said. 'What are we doing? This is as soft as shit. Let's get our heads together and get it right.'

We were doing a tackling drill in which one player holds a bag while the other crashes into it. I was actually holding the bag when my captain came hurtling towards me and hit it with some serious force. I must have had my leg in the wrong spot, because the impact twisted my knee, and I immediately heard a crack. I knew something was seriously wrong, because I couldn't straighten my knee. I hobbled off, and as I drove to Gibbsy's house I was convinced my season was over before it had even started. But straight away Gibbsy unlocked my knee and told me that my cruciate ligament was intact, which was the important thing, but that I would need surgery to fix the damage. This was at 7 p.m. By 6.30 a.m. the next morning I was on the operating table having surgery to repair a tear to the meniscus cartilage in my left knee.

I had already told Gibbsy that I was going to smash all records for the rate of recovery. My aim was to miss just one game and be back playing in round two against Fremantle at the SCG on Sunday week. He thought I was mad and told me that my fellow defender Leo Barry held the record – he was back playing just sixteen days after a similar operation. The thing was I just wanted to play; I just wanted to be there for the boys. I was very much a blokes' bloke and enjoyed being next to them when we went into battle. And when I get something in my head – as my family in particular knows too well – I become manic and can see nothing else. All I could think of at that moment was running onto the ground to play Fremantle.

First of all I had to get out of the hospital, which was going to require a little white lie or two. I was expected to stay in overnight, but I rang Nicole and told her I'd received the all-clear from the doctors and that I'd meet her downstairs in reception. I told the nurse I was going for a walk and put my tracksuit on. I deliberately left all my stuff in the room, because they would have tried to stop me if they'd realised what I was up to. My escape went according to plan and Roosy came around later that night to check up on me. He couldn't believe how twisted I was about my recovery.

'What are you doing checking out of hospital?' he said.

'I'm sweet,' I said. 'I'll be right for next week.'

As soon as I got home I put a compression pump around the knee and started around-the-clock icing to try and get the swelling down. I stayed up all night, and I did it again all the next day and night. I was a freak. I didn't sleep. I just sat on the couch, working on my knee and battling through everything that was coming my way, in particular the ice, which was making my skin painfully cold. I shut everything else out of my life. Nothing else existed. Nicole didn't get a look-in. No one could get in the way of my getting over the injury.

I have always had this blinkered determination to push myself. I remember I played horribly in one pre-season game against Brisbane at Telstra Stadium – I only had three or four touches in the whole match. I left straight after the game, and on the drive home I was going crazy. I was starving, but it was after 11 p.m., so nothing was open. When I got to my last option, KFC, and saw that it was also shut this set me off again. I didn't say a word to Nicole for the entire trip, and I dropped her off at home and drove straight to the club. I went to the gym and just nailed myself on the rowing machine. It was like I had to punish myself for my poor performance. I was doing some handballing and kicking when assistant coach John Longmire walked in. He'd left something in his office and couldn't believe it when he saw me working out.

There was a similar mindset being employed to get over the knee injury, and within a couple of days I was walking.

By Tuesday I was back at training, moving around having a light kick, with a bandage around my the knee the only sign of what I'd been through. I got the all-clear from the medical staff after completing a running session on Thursday and was picked to play.

'It's staggering,' Roosy told the media, who had jumped on the story and were running before-and-after photos, with a timeline of my recovery in the newspaper. Thankfully, I lived up to my part of the bargain and played particularly well, grabbing eighteen possessions and kicking a goal in our thirty-one-point victory.

Another factor in pushing myself to make the most of every game was the sudden death of my friend Cormac McAnallen in Ireland a few weeks earlier. I had been completely dumbfounded when I'd found out that my International Rules teammate had died of a heart attack at just twenty-four. Cormac was an absolute star. He'd just been appointed captain of County Tyrone and had won an All-Ireland medal the year before. He was about to get married and had just finished his degree. More than 15,000 people turned out for his funeral, which says a lot about the high esteem in which he'd been held. His death certainly put a few things in perspective and made me realise that I was lucky to have my health and the opportunity that I'd be given, so I needed to do everything to ensure I made it work.

While my knee held up in the coming weeks, injuries to other players were mounting and we lost four games in a row early in the new season as a result. We steadied midway through the campaign and started to gain momentum, with the round thirteen game against Collingwood at Telstra Stadium a defining one for a number of reasons. Playing against the Magpies was always a big occasion, because they had such a massive following all around Australia. They were easily the most well-known and recognisable AFL team in the country, with a long, proud history of Premiership success. Every time you played them you were guaranteed a bumper crowd, and on this night there were 50,000 people at the stadium. But adding to the hype was the fact that it was the only AFL match on that weekend, as the league had introduced a split-round to give players a midseason break.

I used to always talk up how much I loved the big stage. Well, this time I got to deliver when the spotlight was at its brightest. Collingwood were five points up late in the final quarter, and there were only a couple of minutes remaining when there was a ball-up in the centre of the ground. I followed my opponent, Scott Burns, up to the stoppage and instantly saw that there might be an opportunity to run off. I winked at Goodesy, who was playing on Magpies' captain Nathan Buckley, and signalled that he needed to block for me. Doyley got a beautiful tap down to Jude Bolton, who slipped a quick handball to me, and as I took off Goodesy stepped in front of Burns to cut him off. I had nearly got in front of Buckley when I felt him lunge, getting hold of my shorts with his fingertips and pulling them halfway down. But I was going at full gasket by this stage, so it wasn't enough to stop me. I then took a bounce and let fly from fifty metres as another Collingwood player, Shane Woewodin, dived across in front of me in an attempted smother. The ball wobbled in the air for a while before scraping inside the left-hand goalpost to put us back in front. It was the twenty-third goal of my career but by far the most important and timely.

'That was probably the best goal he has ever kicked, except for a few points in a game of Gaelic football,' Roos said in his after-match press conference. 'To come from Ireland to play in front of 50,000 and kick the match-winner is a phenomenal story.'

Confidence is an amazing thing. While I had begun to feel comfortable on the AFL field over the previous twelve months, in recent weeks I had moved to another level. I was starting to make an impact on the result of games and had a career-high twenty-eight possessions in round twenty. We finished the home-and-away season in sixth place, which meant we didn't have a double-chance, like the previous year, and faced a do-or-die showdown with West Coast at Telstra Stadium. The top four teams at the end of the twenty-two rounds earn the right of a double-chance which means if they lose in the opening week of the finals they remain in the running. However, for teams that finish fifth to eighth, their finals are straight elimination. The home-ground advantage was significant against a team who had to come halfway across Australia, and we capitalised on that, winning easily by forty-one points.

Next was a clash with St Kilda, who were a young team on the rise. They'd had a breakthrough season, finishing third on the ladder, but had been smashed by eighty points in the qualifying final by reigning champions Brisbane. That wasn't exactly good news for us, because there is nothing more dangerous than a humiliated team back on its home patch for Friday night football at the MCG. Unfortunately, the Saints followed the script, and we succumbed badly in the second half, conceding eleven goals to four to end our season with a fifty-one-point thrashing.

I returned to Ireland to play in the International Rules series in October, and, fittingly, we were now playing for the Cormac McAnallen Cup. There was no way in the world that the Ireland team was not going to win the cup in its inaugural year, and we did so quite comfortably, winning both games to take the series by fifty points on aggregate. I then had to return to Australia for the start of pre-season training before getting back on the plane and doing the monster trip all over again for Christmas. There was a little bit of added excitement to my return home that year because my old team, the Listowel Emmets, had made it through to the finals of the county championship. My brother Noel and uncle Mikey were playing, and I jumped at the opportunity to represent my home town again, because it still meant a hell of a lot to me. While it did cross my mind that I should alert the Swans to my activities, given that I had a professional contract with them that was worth around $250,000 a year, I figured it wasn't a big deal, because by training and playing with Listowel I was keeping my body fit and in shape.

The final was on Boxing Day, so we had to limit our normal Kennelly Christmas tradition of drinking Guinness and playing cards until 5 a.m. Our sacrifices paid off, and we won the title, which set off a massive celebration in the town. I really enjoyed giving something back to the community, because no matter where you are you never forget where you come from. The party went on for days, and I was still feeling the effects when I got on the plane a week later for my return to Sydney. What I didn't know then was that someone had let the cat out of the bag in Australia.

On my first day back I was called into a meeting. When I walked into the office I found not only the coach, but the chairman Richard Colless and chief executive Myles Baron-Hay sitting there waiting for me. 'You can't do that, Tadhg,' Myles said. 'You are contracted to us, and what happens if you break your leg or do your knee?' It turned out that my win in Listowel had somehow made it into the papers in Australia.

'I totally understand your position,' I said to the three most powerful people at the football club. 'It won't happen again. It definitely won't happen again.'

I sounded very sincere, but deep down I knew I was lying. If the opportunity to play in a final came about again, I would take it. And it did, twelve months later.

Chapter 9

'We need to get out on the piss.'

I was sitting next to Ben Matthews on the bus as we made our way to Canberra Airport. I'd just played one of the worst games of my career, and the team hadn't been much better. The North Melbourne Kangaroos had run all over us in the last quarter at Manuka Oval, kicking five goals to just three points to win by twenty-three points. While it was only the second round of the 2005 season there was something not quite right with us. Our pre-season form had been average, and it was very un-Sydney-like to cave in like we did against a team that had finished well down the ladder the previous year.

Normally after a bad game my natural reaction was to go on a bender. It was how I dealt with my frustration and disappointment, and this time I felt the team needed some bonding. We spread the word around the boys that we would be having a drink at The Royal at Randwick.

Initially, only four of us turned up, but then a couple more arrived, then there were ten and after an hour or so there were about fourteen of us sitting around chatting about footy. We all knew we'd let ourselves down that day and that things had to change. The more beers that went down, the more people started to open up. One thing we all agreed on was that this group's chance of winning a Premiership was in the next two or three years, so we desperately needed to stop wasting time.

There was a feeling we were getting away from the 'Bloods Code', which had been set up three years earlier. It was like a secret brotherhood, because no one outside of the Swans' players knew about the motto and what it stood for. We were all under strict instructions not to mention it to anyone, especially when doing media interviews. We were to live it, not talk about it.

The genesis of the Bloods was back at the end of 2002 when Roosy took over and our great captain Paul Kelly retired. Aware that there was a leadership vacuum, the new coach brought in renowned consultant Ray McLean, who instigated a programme whereby the players selected a ten-man leadership group to shape the club's values. Stuart Maxfield was appointed captain, and so began a massive cultural change at the club. The basis of the whole thing was honesty, self-sacrifice and no excuses. Everything from that point on was about the team. Egos weren't allowed and those who didn't adhere to the new team focus would soon be weeded out. A document outlining the philosophy of the playing group, containing details about the game plan as well as broader values, was compiled with every player signing off on it. It became known as the Bloods bible.

Any indiscretions were dealt with swiftly by the leadership group. If someone was fifteen minutes late for a recovery session, the whole team was punished. The coaches didn't know anything about the punishment sessions, which regularly involved being at Bondi Beach at 6 a.m. in the morning, rain, hail or shine, carrying two bricks brought from home. These were used in a series of exercises that weren't physically demanding, but the mandatory dip in the chilly, grey ocean was a killer. The early morning sessions weren't about busting your gut; it was more about ramming home the message that everything was now one in, all in.

The Bloods name originated from the South Melbourne Football Club, who had been known as the 'Blood Stained Angels', or 'Bloods' for short, before they became the Swans. It was the perfect motto – the 'Blood Brothers' who abide by the 'Blood' rules.

As much as the new ethos was about trying to get everyone on the same page, it was also about changing the way we were perceived as a team. We wanted teams to dread coming up against Sydney because they knew they were going to be worked over physically and mentally. Part of that was also instilling a belief that we were never out of the game, no matter what the situation, until the final whistle. We had to build a trust and understanding that whatever the circumstances your teammate was there for you, willing to spill blood for the cause.

As the drinks flowed that night and into the early hours of the morning I got the feeling that our season was starting from then. A line had been drawn in the sand, and it was time for us to get back to being the Bloods.

That 'we're never beaten' philosophy was put to the test the following week when we travelled to Brisbane to play the brilliant Lions. For the first three quarters we only managed to kick six goals and were behind by thirty-two-points, but we refused to accept defeat and came back to produce one of the more amazing victories I've been involved in. We kicked seven goals to one, with Hally nailing the match-winner after the siren courtesy of a free-kick he'd been awarded just before it had sounded. It was the only time we'd been in front all night.

Something very frustrating happened in the next three weeks – I was tagged. Opposition teams had come up with strategies to try and stop my run from half-back, which had become my trademark. My opponents were continually taking me out of the play, usually pulling me to full-back, so I was becoming a virtual spectator. I was getting more and more frustrated, and it didn't help that the team had also fallen into a mini-trough. Back-to-back losses at home to Adelaide and Melbourne had followed the Brisbane heroics. We then had to travel to Perth to play West Coast and lost to the tune of forty-five points. I only had ten possessions and immediately sought out Roosy afterwards for some soul-searching.

Ironically, a couple of months earlier my coach had earmarked me as possibly the next superstar of the Swans. 'I think Barry Hall rose last year and Adam Goodes the year before. I think Tadhg Kennelly could possibly do that,' Roos said during the pre-season. 'It's phenomenal what he has achieved already.'

It was nice to hear the coach pumping my tyres up, but so far I was playing nothing like a superstar. There was no simple solution to the first major form slump of my career. I just had to keep working and doing the basic things right and eventually things would turn. The team was told to adopt the same basic philosophy, because with just two wins from six rounds we were looking anything like the Premiership contenders we'd all agreed we were that night at The Royal.

And we were under attack. In an unusual move the AFL's chief executive Andrew Demetriou came out and described our game style as ugly and stated that if we didn't change it, we weren't going to win many more matches. He was concerned that our unattractive brand was hurting the game in the New South Wales market. There were plenty of other people lining up to take a shot at us, with leading commentator Robert Walls one of the most vocal.

This didn't exactly go down well with the club, in particular Roosy, who was furious that his coaching ability was being questioned. While he didn't let it show publicly, the criticism became a key motivational factor in the months ahead and something that the players thrived on.

'The world is against us,' Roosy would often say. 'Look what Demetriou said. No one believes in our game plan. No one believes we can win big games.'

The issue arose because we played a unique style that was very much based on hard, tough, one-on-one, contested football. As a result there were always a lot of stoppages in our games, because we refused to give the opposition an inch. We would scrap and fight for every ball. We weren't a team full of superstars, and, more importantly, we weren't a team full of wankers. We were very coachable, and our strength was our willingness to work for each other, to sacrifice our own game for the team. If that meant locking down and making the match a scrap, that's what we did. I regularly felt I could have done more, could have gone and got another fifteen kicks, as my natural instinct was to attack, but I knew my role was to stay back and do my job for the team. All around the ground we had guys doing exactly the same thing, and it was a strategy and game plan that had got us into two finals series in a row, so the accusation that it wasn't successful didn't wash with Roosy or the players.

There was a fair bit of 'up yours' in the round seven game against Essendon at Telstra Stadium when we came from behind, kicking four goals to one, to claim victory by just six points. The criticism had brought everyone at the club closer together. From the chairman down to the water boy, we were all in this together, and from that night our season really started to roll. We won seven of our next nine games, which included back-to-back one-point wins. In round thirteen we hung on to defeat Collingwood by a point – I had to take the final kick-in with thirty seconds left on the clock, which thankfully I executed properly – at Telstra Stadium. Then the following week we played Richmond at the MCG and came back from forty-six points down in the third quarter to lose by only a point. But the real evidence of how far we'd progressed came in round seventeen when we took down West Coast, who had only lost one game that season, by nineteen points at home and moved into third position on the ladder. Not bad for a team who played ugly football!

Life was going well off the field, with my first real-estate purchase in Australia. House prices in Sydney are unbelievable, much higher than anywhere else in the country, because it's all about location, location, location. I wanted to find somewhere in the Bondi area, which was naturally one of the most expensive. My initial aim was to find something for around $800,000, but Nicole fell in love with a place in North Bondi, which had a price tag of $1,025,000. I couldn't believe I was going to spend a million bucks on a house. I spoke to Mickey O, who was the Swans' house-buying guru. He told me to bite the bullet with my first one, because you're always going to spend more than you want to, and in the long run it would prove to be a wise investment. I was also a bit nervous, because the idea of returning home to Ireland was always at the back of my mind, so I didn't know whether I wanted to get tied down with such a major financial obligation.

I'd already made one venture into house buying back in 2001. I had suddenly found myself cashed up after breaking into the senior team and was thinking of buying a shit-hot car, but my old man wouldn't have a bit of it. Instead, the minute I got home to Ireland we went to Tralee and bought a house. I remember the experience, because it was the first time I really appreciated how much of a legend my father was. On the way home after my purchase we called into a pub in Tralee to have a celebratory pint. Before he could put his hand in his pocket there were people coming over to introduce themselves and say that it would be an honour to buy him a drink. We ended up having lunch and six or seven pints, all of which we were shouted because of the respect people had for Dad. That afternoon always sticks in my mind.

I forgot to tell my new manager Michael that I had bought the house. Given that he was trying to help me set up my financial affairs in Australia that might have been something he needed to know. Since I started, I had steadily risen in the pay ranks, with my contract very much incentive-based. I was rewarded if I played a certain amount of games and by where I finished in the club's best-and-fairest competition each season. There was so much money in the game that the average wage across the entire competition – which was around 640 players – was more than $100,000. The games biggest stars were pushing the $1 million per season barrier, while a first year player starts around $60–70,000 but has the capacity, depending on whether they play senior games straightaway, to earn in excess of $100,000. I was earning way more money than I had ever dreamed of, even when I was fantasising about the extravagant life of a professional as a kid. That didn't mean I spent it freely, and there was a lot of thinking done before I finally agreed with Nicole and Mickey O to make the big purchase.

While it was exciting, in many ways it did signal the end of an era, as we said goodbye to the famous Botany residence. By this stage Scott Stevens had left after being traded to Adelaide at the end of 2003. Ironically, his replacement, Tim Schmidt, was selected by the Swans using the draft pick they'd received from the Adelaide Crows for Scotty. The boys came with me to the new North Bondi house and they were onto me very early about how much I'd changed now that I was the landlord. Certainly, a lot of the shenanigans that went on in the old house were out of bounds given that they were my walls and my furniture!

There was no limit to our confidence in the lead-up to the finals, as we finished the end of the home-and-away season with four impressive victories, setting up a qualifying final showdown (second v. third) with West Coast. They'd suffered a bit of a late-season slump and had been passed by Adelaide, who were playing St Kilda in the other qualifying final. There was a tinge of sadness associated with our brilliant run into the finals, as my idol Stuart Maxfield wasn't going to be there. He'd had a horrible year, resigning from the captaincy earlier in the season for personal reasons and then having a knee injury ruin his campaign.

The final in Perth was one of those nights when I was just on form. I was at the top of my game. Everything I touched turned to gold, and I was convinced we were playing Premiership football. It was a funny sort of game, as we led by as much as fifteen points in the third quarter, but the Eagles would then have a good patch, so the game was up and down all night. The defining moment came midway through the last quarter when the Eagles were handed a goal in one of the worst umpiring decisions I'd ever seen. We had the ball in the back pocket and Leo Barry was running past the West Coast player Tyson Stenglein, who was standing the mark, which is what you do to prevent opposition players from just freely running on when they have either marked or been awarded a free kick. Leo and Stenglein came together and the umpire interpreted it as an illegal shepherd and reversed the kick. He thought Leo was trying to clear a path for his teammate by taking out the West Coast player, when in actual fact Stenglein had moved into Leo. It was totally wrong, with Stenglein given an easy shot at goal, which he slotted through and that was the difference in the end – the Eagles won by four points.

I couldn't believe we'd lost. As soon as I heard the siren my first thought was, 'We have just lost the Premiership.' I knew I couldn't play much better and as a team we'd been brilliant, yet we were now staring at the long road just to make it into the Grand Final. I was still in a state of shock when we got into the changing-room and Roosy called us straight into the small meeting room.

'OK, we've got a short week. We play Geelong next Friday night at home,' Roos said. 'Let's start thinking about how we're going to play them ...'

It was amazing. I had never seen anything like it before. Roosy did not mention anything about what had transpired over the previous couple of hours. He was straight into talking about the following week. He'd already started to discuss match-ups against Geelong, and it was suddenly like the game against the Eagles, which was probably one of the best I'd ever played in, never really happened. It was brilliant coaching.

I thought it might be a while before I played another match with as much drama and tension, but I was very wrong. I only had to wait another six days! The semi-final against the Geelong Cats was an extraordinary game of AFL football. To their credit, the Cats played out of their skins for the first three quarters – we only kicked two goals in the opening half – and when they kicked the first goal of the final quarter their lead was twenty-three points. To just about all of the 39,000 people at the SCG that was the game effectively over. Importantly, there were twenty-two people wearing red-and-white jumpers who didn't think so. That was the beauty of that team: we never believed we were beaten. We never looked up at the scoreboard. We never wondered, 'How are we going to win this?' It was always a case of, 'We *can* win this.' No matter what the circumstances we just had this enormous self-belief that something would happen to turn things around.

That something was Nick Davis.

He was possibly the most talented player on our team, which is saying something given that Goodesy had won the Brownlow Medal in 2003, Hally was the best power forward in the competition and Mickey O was unbelievably skilful. But Davo was simply amazing. He could do things on a football field that no one else could. However, the problem throughout his career had been his dedication to the task. While he wasn't a bad egg, he certainly presented a challenge to Roosy and the leadership to keep him on the right track.

All that patience and effort paid off in twenty minutes of sublime football. The first sign that something special was brewing came midway through the final quarter when Davo timed his run perfectly and ran onto a hit-out by our ruckman Jason Ball. Despite being deep in the forward pocket and on a tight angle, he kicked the ball expertly across his body for a brilliant goal.

Three minutes later he managed to position himself between two Geelong players to mark, twenty metres out, directly in front of our goal. His second goal reduced the margin to nine points with nine minutes remaining. I got in on the act next, getting hold of a loose ball and flicking off a super-quick handball to Davo, who fended off his opponent and screwed the ball around his body from forty metres for another extraordinary goal.

Despite all this we were still behind with the clock closing in on thirty minutes. The umpires had put their whistles away, with players throwing themselves in desperation at the ball whenever they could. We managed to get it into our forward pocket for a ball-up, with every player on the ground inside our forward fifty metres. It was then that the discipline that we had prided ourselves on kicked in. We needed to clear the congestion around the ball-up, so I immediately went to the goal square to pull my opponent out with me, and my teammates followed suit. It was in the spirit of the Bloods, because I was never going to get the ball where I was, but by moving away I was giving our team more of a chance to get it.

I will never forget the next ten seconds. Bally over-powered his Geelong opponent in the ruck and tapped the ball down into the space that had been created on one side of the contest. Running into that space at full speed was Davo, and in one stride he somehow managed to get the ball, which he never really had under control, to his left boot. I was still in the goal square, and I saw the ball sail off his boot, but I wasn't sure whether it had gone through because of the angle I was at until I looked at his face. He'd kicked it. He'd kicked the last four goals of the game to win us the match. I bolted over to him and started jumping around.

Suddenly, we realised that the game wasn't officially over. All of the Sydney players then sprinted to stack our backline, but it didn't matter, as the siren sounded immediately after the umpire bounced the ball in the centre square. Davo's goal had come with just ten seconds remaining in the match.

It was pandemonium after the siren. The crowd went ballistic, the noise was deafening and players were jumping around like we'd won the Grand Final. I did a TV interview on the ground, and there was no way anyone could have understood what I said, because not even I did. I was talking at 100 miles per hour. The changing-room was buzzing once we finally got in there, and I was on real a high when Roosy went to work on us again.

'That was a great win, but we've won nothing yet,' he said. 'Let's keep a lid on it, because we've won nothing. Let's do this properly.'

Almost straight away I felt the room begin to calm down. I certainly started to cool down, as Roosy made it clear that the job was nowhere near finished and that we had a chance to do something really special. Our Premiership dream was still alive.

Chapter 10

We're going to play in the Grand Final!

We're going to play in the Grand Final!

I kept repeating that sentence over and over in my head. The ball was currently in my hands in the back pocket, and I couldn't help but let slip a big smile. There was still ten minutes to go in the preliminary final, but the game was already ours, and I was making sure I enjoyed the moment.

We all knew we had it, but we didn't dare say anything out loud. The nods of the head and the way we were chipping the ball around to take as much time as possible off the clock told me that every Sydney player was thinking exactly what I was.

The previous twenty minutes had been extraordinary. At three-quarter time we were behind by seven points, and everyone at the MCG was expecting St Kilda to follow the script and roll over us in the final quarter. Most of the talk in the press in the lead-up had emphasised that the Swans hadn't won a finals game at the MCG since 1935 and that we were lucky even to be there after scraping through in unbelievable circumstances a week earlier against Geelong.

All season we'd thrived on a 'backs-to-the-wall' and 'us

against the world' mentality, and in the most critical quarter of our season we had channelled it all into an amazing twenty minutes of football. It was total domination by my mate Schneids, who was a goalsneak, a term used to describe a small forward who had the ability to make something happen out of nothing and regularly kick goals from few opportunities. That night he kicked three goals in the quarter as we piled on seven goals to none.

It had been an emotional day for me, with my parents, Noel, his girlfriend Isabelle and my uncle Mikey arriving in Melbourne that morning. Originally, it was only going to be Mum and Dad coming out, but Noel's season with Kerry had been cut short because of injury, so he'd decided to join them, because he knew what a special occasion it was, given I was running out in my hundredth AFL game. Not bad for an Irishman who only really wanted to play one game and go home after two years!

The Swans had a tradition of involving club legends in a ceremony before milestone games, and I was fortunate enough to have my first captain Paul Kelly, who was regarded as one of the most courageous players to have played the game, present me with my jumper.

Kel was back in the changing-room with a lot of other excited people after the match, but things weren't out of control like the week before, because we all knew that this victory – by thirty-one points in the end, with St Kilda not kicking a goal in the last quarter – was just the entrée, with the main course still to come.

I had a strange feeling at the back of my mind: maybe this was all meant to be. Having my hundredth game fall on the preliminary final meant that my family was already there, so there was no last-minute cross-continent dash to get here for the Grand Final. Everything was falling perfectly into place.

I met up with the Kennelly contingent after the game and had a few pints at their hotel. Noel was on good form, and I could have had another twenty but figured that wasn't the best idea. Luckily, they were all exhausted from the trip, so things didn't get out of control. The next morning we all flew back to Sydney, and the club called a meeting of players and partners at the SCG immediately after we arrived to discuss Grand Final week. Luckily for us the man organising everything, operations manager Andrew Ireland, had been through it all with Brisbane during their Premiership run. He knew all the pitfalls and how best to keep the distractions of Grand Final week to a minimum. The biggest problem was tickets, as you could be guaranteed that people you hadn't heard from for months would suddenly come out of the woodwork to ask if you had a 'spare' ticket.

Each player was allocated a certain number of tickets, and the club had organised accommodation in Melbourne for the families, because they would be staying in a different hotel to the players. We all received an itinerary that explained our training schedule and commitments for the week. Every little detail was covered, although I had one minor problem: what was I going to do with my family for the next few days in Sydney?

That night I told them to all bunk down at my house. Mum and Dad could have the spare room and the others would have to sleep on the couch and floor. This meant that all up there were ten of us crammed into my little North Bondi abode, with Doyley and Schmidty, who weren't in the senior team, also in the house. It wasn't exactly the scenario the club wanted, and early the next morning Ireland rang with a solution.

Basil Sellers, the man who had been responsible for bringing me to Australia, was offering one of his apartments in Double Bay for my family. He'd been very supportive from the moment I'd arrived at the Swans and this was just another example of what a great person he was. Mikey, Noel and Isabelle certainly thought so when they arrived at their home for the week. This was *Lifestyles of the Rich and Famous* stuff, with Double Bay regarded as *the* prime real estate in Sydney. The apartment was on the harbour – we're talking six metres from the water – with its own private beach.

After their first night staying there, my father asked Mikey about the new digs. 'Ah, we were kept awake all night,' was Mikey's memorable response.

'Why?' Dad asked.

'The waves kept crashing against the wall of the house and waking me up.'

It was a line he used for the rest of the week when he phoned home to Ireland, and everyone got a great laugh out of it.

On the Wednesday night Basil took us all out to dinner at a very fancy restaurant. There were ten of us there and drinks were flying everywhere, with the girls sipping martinis, even Mum. The bill must easily have been between $2,000 and $3,000. Noel was seated at one end of the table, with Basil down at the other. When our host called for the bill Noel just happened to reach behind him because he had an itch in his back. Basil saw this and mistook it for Noel reaching for his wallet. 'Don't insult me,' Basil bellowed down the table. 'Don't you even think about it.'

Noel cottoned on quickly to what was happening and played it up perfectly. Afterwards he was so pumped that Basil had thought he was attempting to pay when, of course, he had no intention of footing any part of the massive bill. 'He must think I'm the nicest guy in the world because I was the only one who offered to pay,' my elder brother kept saying to wind up the rest of us.

It was great having my family around, because it gave me an important distraction given how Sydney had become gripped with Grand Final fever. This was a bit of a surprise for what was such a mad rugby-league city, but everywhere you went people were talking about the Grand Final and there was a massive media contingent at training sessions.

Behind closed doors, we were keeping everything low-key as we plotted the demise of West Coast, who had defeated Adelaide for the right to play us in the big one. I joked to the media that I would use the All-Ireland-winning experience in my family to help me in the build-up to Saturday.

'My Dad played in eight and won five, and my brother has played in four and won three,' I said to the pack of reporters who'd converged on me before our final training session. 'So I have been able to experience something similar before, a bit of a rehearsal, but I guess I have to experience it for myself now.'

A major part of Grand Final week in the AFL is a parade through Melbourne on the Friday lunchtime. I'd been told it was big, but this was more than big – this was out of control, with 100,000 people lining the streets of the city to cheer us on. I couldn't believe what I was seeing. We were seated in the back of convertibles, which were driven slowly through the maze of people. I was with Darren Jolly, a ruckman who we'd recruited from Melbourne the previous year. TV crews were running alongside the car doing interviews and people were screaming at us from all angles. The parade ended at the Melbourne Town Hall, where both sides were presented on stage alongside the Premiership Cup. The view was incredible, with a sea of red-and-white representing Sydney, while the Eagles fans, dressed in blue and yellow, were also out in big numbers.

It was a magical experience, and it got me thinking that the same thing should be done back at home. In the lead-up to the All-Ireland final the teams are hidden away from everyone. I remember when Noel played in one of his finals he and his teammates caught the train to Dublin the day before the match and were then whisked away in a bus to a secret location. It was stupid wrapping the players in cotton wool and as I looked out at this amazing sight in Melbourne, I couldn't help but think how good it would be to have the same thing through the streets of Dublin.

While there were two interstate teams in the Grand Final there was a lot of support for the Swans in Melbourne because of our links to the old South Melbourne. It had been seventy-two years since the Swans had won a Premiership, so we were being hailed as the drought-breakers, with a lot of the old South Melbourne legends getting involved in the build-up to the final.

After the parade we had a light training session, and while I kept telling myself to try and keep everything as normal as possible, it was difficult not to get caught up with the hype. Everywhere you looked there were flags and posters, with Melbourne gripped by Grand Final fever.

After a team dinner we had a quick chat about our plans for the next day, and then the players were left to their own devices. My phone hadn't stopped buzzing all week, and I'd been forced to turn it off regularly just to try and get some rest. The feedback I was getting from home was that my appearance in the AFL Grand Final on Saturday was big news right across Ireland, and Sky Sports was going to show the game live, beginning at 5.30 a.m. Irish time. My story certainly seemed to have captivated the Australian audience, to the extent that Channel Ten, the TV station broadcasting the Grand Final, had sent a reporter and camera crew to Listowel. They were going to set up in my godfather's pub, O'Carroll's, where Joanne and dozens of relatives and friends were going to be watching the game. It was a busy time in Listowel, because the famous race meeting was on, which saw the town's population swell to around 20,000. Adding to that, Kerry was playing in the All-Ireland final against Tyrone on the Sunday.

I slept as well as could be expected and was up early, but spent most of my time pacing the room waiting for the hours to pass. Luckily, I had turned my phone off, because when I switched it back on I had thirty-five messages.

When I flicked on the TV I got an unexpected surprise, with the faces of some of my old schoolmates taking up the screen. Channel Ten was already doing live links to their reporter, Andy Maher, in Listowel. I texted the boys, telling them to give me a wave just before they were interviewed. 'What would you say to Tadhg right now?' Maher asked.

'Well actually, we just got a text from him now. He's in his hotel room, bored shitless.'

It was a strange feeling watching my sister, grandmother and auntie on TV, and I immediately rang Mum and Dad to make sure they were watching. I then went over to see them and had a quick catch-up. The nerves were starting to build, and Dad pulled me aside for a quiet word as I was about to leave. He wanted me to relax and keep my routine as normal as possible. When we were kids he'd always told us not to play the game before we went out, and there were a couple of occasions I'd come done this in my junior days and then wished I could have had my time over again. That couldn't happen today.

As we shook hands he pulled me in close and told me something I'd heard many times before but for some reason hadn't really understood until that moment: 'Don't let the occasion pass you by.'

CHAPTER 11

My coach was looking at me strangely. I'd just looked up at the massive crowd and had started to laugh. 'Holy fuck. This is awesome,' I said.

Roosy let out a big smile of his own. 'Good to see you're tuned in,' he said.

'Oh man, I'm well tuned in.'

We were standing in front of a giant banner which the Sydney cheer squad had just erected. This was an Aussie tradition, with each club having a group of diehard fans who would spend hours constructing a banner out of crepe paper for the players to run through before the start of every game. The Grand Final edition was a huge blur of red and white with an inspirational message written across it.

I didn't take in what it said, because I was still getting over the roar which had greeted us as we emerged from underneath the stand. It was deafening, and the number of people in the stadium was staggering. All week I had gone out of my way to enjoy the occasion, soak everything up, because I might never get another chance. Previously, I'd been too wound up and had locked myself away in the lead-up to big games. That didn't work, and this way was far more enjoyable and hopefully would be more successful.

As I continued to look around the amazing stadium I said to Roosy, 'This is where I want to be. This is unbelievable.'

During the warm-up I scanned the crowd, because I knew roughly where my parents and brother were sitting. I was struggling to find them until I saw an Irish flag appear behind the goals. They were all standing up waving. I gave them a quick wave back.

I was so glad the waiting was nearly over. The previous couple of hours, after arriving at the ground, had seemed to go on for ever. The entertainment before the game had been like a rock concert, which was a bit different to the old marching band back at home. While it had sounded pretty good, the problem was that it had meant that our normal pre-game routine had been affected and we'd had to do things differently. The waiting had made me increasingly anxious, but I'd kept repeating Dad's words in my mind. At one stage I'd hidden in the trainer's room and had a ten-minute sleep on one of the massage tables just to calm everything down.

Now I was feeling great and confident that the next two and a half hours would go according to plan, because I trusted my teammates to make sure they did. We were a team in every sense of the word, and while that might sound simplistic it was actually something that was very difficult to achieve. I had never met a more unselfish playing group who were prepared to sacrifice a part of their game for the good of the team.

As we started to get into place for the national anthem, I looked around at the men I was going into battle with. Standing proudly out in front was Brett Kirk. He epitomised everything we were about. He sacrificed his own game to focus on stopping the opposition's most dangerous midfielder, and he did it with sheer heart and determination. Kirky was anything but a natural footballer, and he'd been forced to fight all the way just to make it in the AFL, which is why he played every game like it was his last. Since the retirement of Stuart Maxfield, he'd been the one who'd driven the Bloods culture and was the spiritual leader of the team.

Hally was captain for the Grand Final. Since Stewie had resigned, the club had rotated the captaincy between Hally, Kirky and full-back Leo Barry. Our gun centre half forward was actually fortunate to be there for the final, as he'd been suspended for punching St Kilda's Matt Maguire in the stomach during the preliminary final, but luckily had the decision overturned on appeal. Bazza wasn't a big talker, but he led by example and was a real focus for us. If he played well, the Swans generally won. Plus, if you looked at teams that had won Premierships over the years, they all had a quality key-position forward, someone who could take a big grab, kick goals and have a significant physical presence. He was our man and a big scary one at that.

Next was Goodesy, who was by far our most attacking player. He reaped the rewards of the work done by taggers such as Kirky, Crouchy and Ben Matthews, who were charged with locking down the opposition. In a way Goodesy and I were probably the only two attacking players in our team, because just about everyone else played a shutdown role. He was tall, flashy and extremely agile, which attracted the attention of the umpires and resulted in him winning the Brownlow Medal. It was great for us that he won, because it showed that what we did worked and that you could still get individual accolades in such a team-orientated environment.

Then there were the all-important veterans of the team in Paul Williams and Jason Ball, who'd both started their careers elsewhere. Williams was an extremely quick midfielder who played 189 games with Collingwood before moving to Sydney in 2001, while ruckman Ball had played in West Coast's 1994 Premiership-winning side before moving to the other side of the country. They were great at saying the right things at the right time. They were cool characters who could bring the group to order if things were getting out of control.

Ryan O'Keefe, or 'Pebbles' as he was known, was further down the line, and he'd been the hero of the preliminary final. A stylish left-footer, I had never seen anyone train as hard as he did. He was very individual in his preparation and he would do anything – I mean he'd go to the end of the world – to train and get himself right. He was a great player and it showed in his work rate on the ground.

Every man in red and white had a trait that made him special and the team better. I knew that I didn't want to let any of the boys down, and I could guarantee that was the same way they felt. It was the Bloods way.

As usual I had Schneids next to me for the anthem, which I ignored, instead mumbling a few bars of Ireland's national song. Both teams were lined up facing each other and you could sense the tension, with some players trying to stare down their opponents while others fidgeted or looked down at the ground. By now we were all sick of the preliminaries. It was time to get down to business.

When the moment we'd all been waiting for arrived – the bounce of the ball in the centre circle to signal the start of the Grand Final – the adrenalin pumping through my veins was intense. Players came from everywhere to attack the opening bounce, and the umpire quickly called for a ball-up. Second time around, the Eagles cleared it, and their centre half-forward Ashley Hansen marked the ball unchallenged as he led up from the forward line. I followed my opponent, Andrew Embley, down towards the goals and read Hansen's kick perfectly, cutting across to take a mark in front of the Eagles' full-forward, Michael Gardiner. It was so good to get my hands on the ball in the opening minute and, more importantly, I had taken it cleanly. After dishing off a handball, I followed the play down the wing and managed to find space. Although Pebbles' kick to me was very close to the boundary line, I somehow managed to keep the ball in. I then took off, but, unfortunately, my kick finished in between two Sydney players. I wasn't happy with that, but the fact I'd had two touches early was promising.

While I'd been telling myself it was just another game I soon realised after the first five minutes that for me it wasn't. I couldn't believe it, but I was seriously struggling, gasping for air. The release of all the tension that had built up through the week and on the day of the match had drained my energy.

Why is this so hard? Come on. Where's my second wind? Is it coming?

Thankfully, the ball didn't come my way for a few minutes while I tried to gather my senses. The Eagles had got the first goal, but Darren Jolly replied quickly for us from a free kick after a ruck contest. Luckily, by the ten-minute mark I'd come good. Everything had calmed down and I was back in normal working order. This was lucky, because it was my responsibility to kick the ball in after behinds had been scored. This was one of the most stressful aspects of the game, as any turnover from the kick-in usually resulted in a goal to the opposition. It was a massive thing for me that I'd been given the responsibility and it showed how far I'd come. I was chosen ahead of guys who'd been kicking the ball all their life.

Our lead was two points at quarter-time, but we turned it up a notch in the second quarter, quickly securing a twenty-point advantage. The highlight for me was my second goal of the year, and it was a reward for aggressive running. The play started in our back pocket and I sensed there was a chance to create something, so I took off. I'd run nearly 100 metres from one end of the field to the other when Sean Dempster chipped the ball over to me. I marked and went back for the set-shot, which was on a tight angle, but I was only twenty-five metres out.

Just do the same thing you do every time. This is just a normal game. Kick the fucking goal!

The second it left my boot I knew it was a goal. I'd hit it perfectly and had one fist in the air before the ball had gone through the posts. I got plenty of high-fives from my teammates on the way back to my position at the other end of the ground. It was amazing to kick a goal in the Grand Final.

At half-time the game was ours to lose, as the Eagles had failed to score a goal in the second quarter, and the scoreboard was looking good: 6.3 (39) to 2.7 (19). The low score said a lot about the pressure of the occasion, because the weather conditions were perfect for football yet goals were hard to come by.

There was a lot of encouraging going on at half-time. We knew that if we kept our level of intensity up, we were only just over an hour away from winning the Premiership. The signs were good, with most of our big guns having been involved in the first half. Hally, Goodesy and Kirky had enjoyed significant touches, while a couple of our lesser names, including tall defender Lewis Roberts-Thompson and Nic Fosdike, were playing the games of their lives.

Roosy's final words were, 'Look, you don't want to come back in twenty years' time and remember you were one hour away from winning a Premiership. You don't want to be thinking, "If only I had done this. If I only I had given an extra bit. If only, if only."'

The spring in our steps didn't last very long, as it was obvious from the opening minutes of the third quarter that the Eagles had come out with a more aggressive and attacking attitude. Errors that weren't there in the first half were creeping into our game. At one stage I went to take off on a run but left the ball behind and had to go back to get it. Little things like that were putting us on the back foot. I knew we had problems when midway through the quarter I beat my opponent, Daniel Chick, to the ball, but the stupid thing bounced sideways on me, like a rabbit as I used to call it, and into the hands of Hansen, who turned around and snapped a goal for the Eagles. Then, when I decided to try and create something up front and found myself in space a few minutes later, Schneids' kick was too short and was easily intercepted by the Eagles. If it had been a couple of feet higher, I would have had an easy shot at goal for my second of the day. But that summed up the quarter. Our lead had been whittled back to just two points, and this time it was us who'd failed to score a goal in the period.

While the situation had suddenly became a lot tighter, Roosy still had his usual air of calmness at three-quarter time, and as a group we knew we'd been in a similar situation many times before and had always found a way out. As we were about to leave the huddle Kirky called all the players in again. 'Let's just give it every fucking thing we've got.' Our spiritual leader was eyeballing every one of us. 'We might never be back here again, so for the next thirty minutes just give it everything.'

I had yet another opponent for the final quarter, this time goalsneak Ashley Sampi. He was the type of player who only needed an inch of space to manufacture a goal, so I had to be on my toes. Unfortunately, my teammate, Luke Ablett, wasn't on his when he handed West Coast the lead, kicking the ball across goal towards Leo in the opposite pocket, but only managing to get it as far as Eagles star Ben Cousins. The champion midfielder, who earlier in the week had won the Brownlow Medal, went back and slotted the easiest of goals. I was the first one over to Ablett to give him a pat on the back, because he needed to put the shocking error out of his mind. 'Don't worry, mate. Everyone makes mistakes,' I said. 'We'll be right.'

That confidence was tested a couple of minutes later when the Eagles scored another goal, this time through Adam Hunter. The margin was now ten points with a bit over ten minutes remaining. But still there was no panic, I suppose partly because the Geelong win was very much still in our minds. Hally marked and scored a goal on the lead shortly afterwards to get us back within a kick, and Mickey O then had another shot, but, unfortunately, his radar had been off all day and he missed badly again.

With seven minutes and forty-two seconds left we produced another special moment and this time it was Amon 'Monty' Buchanan who delivered. Once again it was a brilliantly orchestrated set-play at a ball-up, with Bally hitting it into the space that had been kept free through the discipline of our players to take their opponents away from the contest. Monty then came steaming into the gap, gathered the ball, ducked underneath a tackle and slammed through a quick goal on his left foot. It was a textbook play and we were now one point up.

From the centre bounce the Eagles went forward, but I managed to cut out the play by using my soccer skills to release the ball. I then picked it up and took a bounce as I tore along the wing. My kick went deep into the forward pocket, where I hoped the ball might stay for the next five minutes. We clearly had the momentum, but kept missing opportunities to close down the game. Jude Bolton kicked a point, and then O'Keefe and Williams also scored behinds. Then, with the clock nearly at the thirty-minute mark, Goodesy missed a goal, instead scoring another behind, which meant our lead was up to five points.

That's not enough to be safe. Shit.

The Eagles quickly brought the ball back in, and suddenly they were running at us in waves. This had to be their final attack and they knew it, with players coming at us from every angle. The ball was sent long into their forward line and luckily, out of the corner of my eye, I saw him. The ball had floated over the back of the pack and was bouncing dangerously towards West Coast's goal, with one of their players, Mark Nicoski, sprinting towards it.

C'mon Tadhg, run.

Fortunately, I had enough of a break to beat him to it and safely carry the ball through for a behind. As I pulled up against the fence I couldn't help but let out a massive smile to the Swans' supporters who were screaming at me.

Surely, I had just won us the Grand Final?

I knew there was no way this Sydney team was going to lose possession now. The clock on the scoreboard was past thirty-two minutes and we were four points up, 58 to 54. It was my responsibility to kick in and even though this was going to be the most important kick of my life, I felt surprisingly calm.

An option quickly became available in the back pocket with Leo out there on his own. Normally, he wouldn't be my preferred option but late in the game we'd been drilled to always go to the back pocket and then either open up the space at half-back to hit a teammate on the lead or kick long down the boundary line and get the ball out of bounds. Thankfully my fifteen-metre kick hit its target and straight away I bent over and put my hands on my knees. I was exhausted.

As I looked up, I saw Goodesy get himself clear and make a good lead towards Leo, but he clearly wasn't going to trust himself to pinpoint a pass at such a crucial time so instead he kicked it long down towards the boundary line. That looked fine as our ruckman Darren Jolly had front position against his opponent Dean Cox.

NOOOOOOOOOOOOOOOOO!

In a split second my body was gripped with panic. Cox had worked Jolly under the ball and marked it.

Where the hell is my man?

I looked up and the ball was coming straight towards Sampi.

Like a dog on heat, I sprinted straight for him, grabbing hold of his jumper.

I don't care what happens but one thing I can guarantee you Sampi, you're not going to be the hero.

Next thing I knew, I was on the ground after copping what felt like an elbow to the head. There were three Eagles' players around me but I knew something big had just happened. Someone had taken a mark. The crowd was going crazy. I knew it wasn't Sampi because I'd dragged him down with me when the pack converged on us. I turned around and couldn't believe my eyes. There was Leo with the ball in his hands.

You legend!

As I staggered towards him rubbing my head, I heard it. The sound which I'd been waiting to hear for what had seemed like an eternity finally infiltrated my senses – the siren.

We've won. We've fucking done it.

I jumped on Leo and buried him into the MCG turf. I screamed 'I love you' into his ear as teammates came flying over and piled on top of us. It had been seventy-two years since the Swans had won the Premiership and we'd done it now in the most dramatic circumstances.

The next few minutes were complete mayhem as the celebrations began. There were kisses, hugs and tears going everywhere. It was an amazing feeling. Soon, my thoughts drifted to my family and the people back home in Ireland. Luckily my mother, father, brother and uncle had got to witness this in person and I knew my sister would be going crazy back in my godfather's pub. My train of thought was broken when I heard the announcer call my name: 'Number 17, Tadhg Kennelly'.

Each player, in numerical order, got called onto the stage where they received their Premiership Medal with the captain and coach called up last and presented with the Premiership Cup.

Right now, I am the proudest Irishman on the planet. I am so proud of what I've achieved and what it means to my country. Can you believe it, an Irishman has won an AFL Premiership Medal? Six years ago I hadn't even picked up an Aussie football, yet here I am on the biggest sporting stage in Australia. What can I do?

Just before I walked through the maze of people to get to the stage, I told Nic Fosdike about my plan. He smiled and gave me a high-five. It was the perfect message to send home to everyone watching in Ireland.

Once the medal was placed around my neck, I turned and looked around at the 91,828 people in the stadium and started dancing – doing an Irish jig just like I would if I was home in Listowel.

Chapter 12

The moment I saw him I felt it coming. As my father wrapped his big arms around me and drew me in, I knew I could no longer hold back the emotion. Despite all the celebrations and excitement going on around me I was crying. And so was my Dad.

I had managed to pull my family into a corner away from everyone, as the changing-room was packed with media and supporters. Mum got a picture of my moment with Dad, and then we did a group hug before I grabbed a few Crown Lagers and slumped against the wall with my old man and brother.

Right at that moment I was the happiest man in the world. I'd reached the pinnacle in my chosen sport, done something that no Irishman had ever done before, done something that almost everyone thought I couldn't do, and my family were there with me to enjoy it. I'd already spoken to my sister and grandmother out on the ground, because Channel Ten had done a live link to Listowel. Reporter Neil Cordy had been holding a tiny TV, so I'd been able to see them all jumping around in O'Carroll's. It had been surreal talking to them in the middle of the MCG with a Premiership Medal around my neck.

The lap of honour after the presentations had been an unforgettable experience. I'd wanted it to last forever. The outpouring of emotion had been overwhelming, with so many people bursting with joy. It had been incredible, and at one stage I'd hopped up on a fence with Mickey O to get the crowd dancing. I'd managed to snare an Irish flag and scarf from someone and had proudly brandished them around the ground.

Once we finally got downstairs, Roosy pulled us all into the small meeting room so we could have some time on our own before the mayhem outside hit us. It was a great idea. We put the Premiership Cup in the middle of us all and cracked our first beers, naturally taking turns to drink out of the cup. Sitting there and chatting to the boys, reflecting on the biggest day of our lives, was simply priceless. We were in there for only fifteen minutes, but if I could bottle something from the day, it would be that. The bond the twenty-two players now had would last for ever.

Eventually, the media found us hidden away, and they asked Dad how he was feeling. 'What can I say? It's just a fairy tale,' he said. 'I've witnessed finals at home, having played in them, but this is just unreal.

'Tension? There was fierce tension. I have a bit of a heart condition, and I can tell you one thing: it must be a very, very good one to get through that and still be ticking. It was just beautiful. It's a dream come true for us.

'We're delighted and very proud of Tadhg. He's very level-headed. He came over here six years ago and we thought he faced a mighty test. His mum didn't want to let him go, but after a while we had to give in to him.

'He has worked so hard, the coaches have told me. He'd be there an hour before training and stay an hour after it just to pick up things that he had to learn. I'm very proud of him.'

Despite it being about an hour since I'd won an AFL Premiership Medal the questions were flying thick and fast about when I would be returning to Ireland to chase an All-Ireland medal. 'I'll definitely head home. I don't know when,' I said. 'It's still a big part of my life, and I want to do it, but I don't want to think about that right now. I want to savour and enjoy this moment for as long as I can.'

The partying started at the official dinner at the Crown Casino, with the Swans' theme song belted out what seemed like every few minutes. Dressed in suits but with our jumpers over the top we were all individually presented to the 1,300 people in the massive ballroom. It was like being a rock star, and it actually got a bit much later on, with people constantly coming up to our table asking for autographs and photos. To escape it all Schneids and I hid under the table, and for about forty-five minutes we sat down there and asked our families to keep feeding us drinks.

Once the formalities were over the band came in and I was immediately called up onto the stage, because everyone wanted to see my jig again. I agreed to do it, but on one condition. Pop star Delta Goodrem, who was a friend of Jude Bolton's and had been a lifelong Swans club member, was there with her boyfriend, Irish singer Brian McFadden. I wanted McFadden to come up on stage and belt out an Irish tune. He did, and the crowd went nuts, particularly my Mum, who loved him. We made sure she got a photo with her favourite singer.

The club had organised a function in a nearby pub for players and family only, and it was great to escape there after the official dinner had ended and just relax. I decided the occasion warranted a cigar, even though I had never tried one before in my life. I had it in my mouth for the next five hours.

There was no chance the night was going to end there and we eventually ended up back at the Crown Casino, at one of the nightclubs with some of the West Coast players. Sampi was there, and we had a joke about the final seconds when he should have got a free kick before Leo came over the top of us to take the match-winning mark.

'You ripped off the 2005 AFL Grand Final logo on my jumper,' Sampi said.

I cracked up. 'C'mon, brother. I would never commit a foul. I'm the cleanest fella out there.'

We were still going strong as the sun rose, and a combination of lots of singing, shouting and the cigar meant my voice was just about gone. Somehow Hally, Schneids, Noel, my uncle Mikey and myself made it back to the team hotel at about 8.30 a.m. We had no intention of going to bed, and Andrew Ireland met us in the lobby and said that the bus was leaving in twenty minutes. The plan was to attend a supporters' function in Port Melbourne, near the Grand Prix track, and then go from there to the airport and back to Sydney. The football operations boss soon figured out we weren't going to venture very far from our seats in the lobby, so he went up and packed our bags for us.

Thank God for sunglasses! They saved my life at the meet and greet with the fans, because I was able to hide some of the pain I was beginning to feel. Although losing my voice got me out of making any speeches, I once again had to do my Irish jig. I was beginning to realise that I was going to be remembered more for that than actually playing in the game.

While the reception in Melbourne had been big it was nothing compared to what awaited us at the SCG that afternoon. The ground and the stands were a sea of red and white. There were people everywhere and it was quite overwhelming. The next few hours were a blur of photos, autographs and more drinking.

I finally got some sleep that night – most of it in the cab on the way home – but we were at it again for 'Mad Monday' at the Annandale Hotel. We met in the function room at 11 a.m., but this celebration was strictly for players and coaches only, which meant there were no rules. Blokes were dressed up in all sorts of gear, with weird and wonderful behaviour the order of the day.

The only slight disappointment was that I wasn't celebrating two wins, with Kerry losing by three points to Tyrone in the All-Ireland final: 1–16 to 2–10. Twice the Kingdom had fought back to get within a point, but it wasn't to be.

After a few more days of partying and lots and lots of laughing and singing, we took part in a ticker-tape parade down George Street in the city. While I'd been blown away by a lot of things over the past six days the sight of 100,000 people packing the streets of Sydney to celebrate the performance of an AFL team – remember, it is very much a rugby-league town – was massive. Mickey O and I were in the back of a car as confetti and red-and-white streamers rained down on us from office windows.

The impact of our win was enormous on the city of Sydney. The previous night Davo and I had appeared with the Premiership Cup on rugby league's highest-rating TV programme *The Footy Show*. This was something the hierarchy at the Swans thought they would never see, given that the two sports had always been bitter rivals. Sydney was a tough market to crack, and the two codes were constantly battling each other for a share of the corporate dollar.

Mum and Dad were the only ones left by the end of the week, and I was due to fly back to Ireland with them after the Swans best-and-fairest night. This was to be the final official celebration, but the big week of partying was starting to take its toll. Nevertheless, we all managed to get up for my last crack at a party. I came sixth behind Kirky and was pretty happy with my highest-ever finish. I'd also received eight Brownlow votes for the year, which was a good stat.

We were going to have company on the way home, with Fox Sports sending over a camera crew and reporter, Tiffany

Cherry, to report on my homecoming. She'd been to Ireland twelve months earlier and filmed a documentary entitled *Torn Between Two Codes* about my journey to Australia. She didn't get much good footage on the plane, because I was in bits. However, the Premiership win was already producing some perks, with me, Mum and Dad being upgraded to first class by Qantas. It was an inspired move by Australia's national airline – they had me for life after that. The time to relax got me to reflecting a bit on the enormity of what I'd done, but I figured it would hit home more once I was back where it had all started.

Once I did hit Irish soil, all I wanted to do was sit in a quiet corner of one of my local pubs and have a couple of pints with a few of my close friends. I told Dad as much on the drive home from the airport, but he said we should get something to eat before we got to Listowel, and he needed to go to the toilet urgently. We were just outside Tarbert, which was about twenty minutes from home, and he was so insistent about the toilet stop that Mum stopped at Kirby's Lanterns Hotel.

I begrudgingly got out of the car to stretch my legs, and as soon as I took one step inside the pub I realised I'd been set up. The bar was packed with more than fifty family and friends. My father had arranged for them to come to the pub because he figured it would be mayhem in Listowel. This way I got to spend a couple of quality hours with those closest to me. It was a cracking idea, but Dad wasn't finished with his little tricks.

As we drove through the village of Tarbert on the way home we came across heaps of people standing alongside the road. I figured it was a funeral procession, but Dad told Mum to pull over. 'We're getting out here,' he said.

'Like fuck we are. I'm not getting out. It's a fucking funeral.'

'Just get out of the car.'

Again, I didn't realise what he was up to, but the moment I opened the door and started to get out of the car all the people started cheering. There wasn't any funeral. They had come out to see me. I couldn't believe it. This wasn't even my home town, and yet there were people going bananas about what I'd done. I was blown away.

We eventually got out of Tarbert and made it home, where I collapsed on the couch before heading for the shower. I had rung my mates and told them I'd be down at Christie's pub in an hour or so. Dad said he'd drop me there but had to make a detour on the way. 'I just need to go up to the football field for a second,' he said.

By now I was suspicious of his every move, and I knew he was up to something again, because there were people all over town. I was proved right, as there was a truck at the football field, which I was apparently going to sit on top of to be paraded through the main street. I couldn't believe what everyone was doing for me. As we edged our way towards the town square there were thousands of people lining the streets, with the gardaí blocking off traffic for my truck. It was like I was the president.

A stage had been erected in the square and Tom Walsh, the Listowel mayor, welcomed me before I got the chance to thank everyone. I had my Premiership Medal around my neck, and I could feel myself getting emotional. 'This is unbelievable,' I said. 'I said to someone yesterday before I left Sydney that it was the best week and last Saturday probably the best day of my life, but this goes miles and miles past it. This is by far the best night, the best day, of my life, so thank you all very much.

'It's basically this town that has driven me. All the time I have been away, but more so when I was a young fella here, there was this drive to be a proud Listowel and Kerry man, a proud Irishman. This town is so close-knit, and there is such a great family feel about the place. That is what really drives me when I am on the other side of the world, and in the last three or four minutes of the game in the Grand Final I remember thinking to myself, "What am I going to do if we lose, because everyone will be very disappointed and I'll have let the town down." It's something that drives me. I never want to feel like I have let the town down, never be a failure.'

Then Walsh asked me the question that was on everyone's mind. 'Have you got ambitions to come back in the future?' he said.

'Definitely. I think a lot of people were disappointed that I did leave in 1999. I have said all along that hopefully the next time I am standing up here it's with an All-Ireland medal for Kerry. It's something that drives me, and I probably went out to Australia initially to learn to be a better Gaelic footballer coming back. It's something I have always wanted to do, and a part of my life will always be missing if I don't win an All-Ireland. It's something I am definitely going to do, or try to do anyway.'

Dad then followed me up to the microphone. 'I came here in 1979 with the Sam Maguire for the first time, and it was an honour. It's a bigger honour here tonight to speak on behalf of my family for what Tadhg has done in Australia,' he said. 'I would sincerely like to thank all you people, young and old, who have turned up here tonight, not only from Listowel but from all over Kerry. Thank you very much.'

My idea of a few quiet beers was out the window, as I was being mobbed like a rock star. The attention was overwhelming. Kids were chanting my name and everyone wanted a photo, a kiss, a hug or to touch the medal. It was the start of more madness, with everyone wanting a piece of me. There were interview after interview requests, appearances and even a civic reception put on by the town's council.

The following day I was on Radio Kerry and was asked a question that struck a chord and had me thinking about the reason why my world had changed for ever: 'Why did the Swans win this year?'

'We were very much an underdog to win the Premiership this year, and basically we played for each other, played for each other just to get the respect of each other,' I replied. 'I suppose when it comes down to it that's how you win games. We were a champion team not a team of champions.'

Paul Roos

'I remember probably the biggest adjustment he had to make when he started playing was adapting to the physical nature of the game. With his size it was about getting used to contact, because they're just not used to it in the Gaelic game. It's such a shock to them, and that was probably the thing that stood out with me. I don't think anyone questioned that he could make it in an athletic sense and even in terms of his skills, but I think the biggest thing was how would he adjust to the physicality of the game.

'The thing that really sticks out for me more than anything with Tadhg is his absolute determination. As well as being senior coach I have also been his direct coach. I would sit with three or four of the senior players and watch videos of their performances each week. Tadhg would cringe at what he saw. He got embarrassed by some of the things that he saw himself doing, and I knew it was just his professionalism. He needed to see it, but he could barely watch himself doing something that he didn't like. I could see his blood boiling, and I knew he would play well the following week because he just couldn't bare the thought of doing the same thing again, whether it be a bad kick or a missed tackle. In a team meeting – and we were pretty honest with our players – if something he had done wrong was being shown on video, I would watch him, and he wouldn't be dirty with me for putting it up there, he would be dirty with himself. He would be so hard on himself. He would almost get up and walk out, because he just hated watching himself do something wrong in front of the team.

'He was such a professional, and his commitment was absolute because he had given up so much to come. He was never, ever going to leave without knowing that he had given absolutely everything. That is why he used to play with shoulder injuries and knee injuries, all those sorts of things when other blokes wouldn't play, because he had sacrificed so much. I'm sure in his own mind he was thinking, "Well, I can't not play because I have given up my family. There is no way I am not going to play this week, because I have given up so much to be here. I am here. I am going to be successful. I am going to make my family proud." I love him as a person, but the real thing that stands out for me is that his determination to be successful was extraordinary.

'If I had to pick the two most determined players I've ever seen, it would be Kirky and Tadhg. They would be equal with each other in terms of their determination to be successful.

'Tadhg was a great decision-maker, which is amazing, as he went from a guy who had never kicked an AFL ball to being probably our best kick and decision-maker. His three greatest attributes were his ability to read the play, his decision-making and his skill execution.

'He got tagged in a Grand Final, he had an opposition forward try to sit on him and follow him everywhere, which is amazing when you consider he was an Irishman who'd only come out to play Aussie rules a few years earlier. He did things in handball games or when we were trying to work our players through the opposition zones at training that most of our other guys couldn't do. In traffic he would just weave his way through and hit a target, whereas other blokes would get tackled and fumble the ball and kick it to the opposition.

'People talk about champion players and great players. I think the mark of a great player is their ability to play with injuries. I think that is huge and I don't think you can ever be considered a great player if you can't play with injuries. Tadhg was equal to any of the guys I have played with or seen in terms of being able to play with injury.

'When his Dad passed away we gave him as much time as he needed to go home and get his house in order and make sure that he was emotionally able to come back. To be perfectly frank it wouldn't have surprised us if he'd said that he wasn't able. It just goes back to his absolute determination. I'm sure his family would have said, go back, your Dad wouldn't want you to come home, go and finish what you have started over there. If it was possible, his determination, his competitiveness and drive, continued to grow and grow. It was even greater after the loss of his father. He wasn't going to waste a minute, he wasn't going to waste a training session, he wasn't going to waste a game, a quarter or whatever it was.

'I could sense it in the end when he wanted to go back. He was so proud of his performances, and I knew that he didn't want to go back and be a bit player in Ireland. I've no doubt that he thought he could still contribute in the AFL, but his real concern was getting injured again and not being able to go back and fulfil what he wanted to do back in Ireland.

'Some of the criticism about the timing of his decision was extra-ordinary. The thing is, if he rang me tomorrow and said he wanted to come back, I'd take him back. I love all my players, but there are some with whom you feel a special bond, and I would pick him tomorrow, because I know he would die for me. I would take him back in a heartbeat.

'The other thing I loved about Tadhg was that he was always positive. I could give other blokes a roasting and they would slide past your office and try not to be seen. Tadhg, on the other hand, regardless if we won by forty points or lost by forty points, was just a very level-headed person.

'He is a great person and a great footballer. I enjoyed his company. I used to love him coming into my office and talking about Gaelic footy. I used to joke with him that Jack O'Shea still owes me money from the lesson I gave him when I played in the Gaelic footy back in Ireland in 1987.

'I think we tend to be a little bit blasé over here about what he achieved. But there are very few blokes who play in Premierships, let alone an Irishman. I have been to Ireland and played at Croke Park. I have been around the world. I have been fortunate enough to go to Wimbledon, the French Open, the Super Bowl and the Major League Baseball All-Star Game. The AFL Grand Final is on a par – it's a massive event. I don't think Tadhg fully realised that until he was actually part of it. He didn't really know what it was going to be like and then all of a sudden he was on the big stage and playing such a significant part in a Premiership win.

'Tadhg was one of the few game breakers we had. He was actually a massive weapon. When you look at the sum of our parts in 2005 we probably could have won it without such and such a player or such and such, but I know we couldn't have won it without Tadhg. His best finish in the best-and-fairest might have been fifth or sixth, but if you look at his legacy to the Sydney Swans Football Club, it's significant. If you really sat down and analysed it, if you were doing a thing in twenty years on the Swans 2005 Premiership and you were to really break it down, you would say that Kennelly, the Irishman, was one of the most important people involved in the Swans' success. No question.'

Chapter 13

A piercing sound jolted me from my sleep. I immediately sat upright, but it took me a couple of seconds to realise what it was. The fire alarm had gone off, but that couldn't be right, as I was sure it didn't work. In fact I was positive we'd disconnected it because it had kept going off. I met Doyley in the hallway, and we were both perplexed at how the alarm, which was barely hanging onto the roof, was still making that annoying beeping sound. My seven-foot tall housemate then reached up and pulled out the battery for good.

When I got back to bed, Nicole asked if the house was on fire, but I assured her everything was fine. The whole episode was very strange.

An hour later my sleep was interrupted again, this time by Nicole's mobile phone ringing. It was almost 2 a.m., and I wondered who'd be calling her at that hour?

'What's happened?' I heard Nicole say. 'What's happened?' Her face had gone pale, and she handed me the phone without saying a word. I knew straight away it was Dad.

The voice at the other end was Noel's.

'Dad's gone,' he said.

'No!' I screamed. I felt my body go limp as tears started streaming down my face. I tried to ask my brother what had happened but could barely get the words out.

It turned out that Dad's heart had stopped when he was at home, and Joanne had found him. Noel had been at work, and Isabelle had rung him and told him that there had been 'an accident' and to get around to my parents' house as soon as possible. He had no idea what had happened until he arrived. He then realised that Mum wasn't there. She didn't know what had happened and had gone out without her mobile phone, so there was no way of contacting her. By this stage the word was already starting to spread through town, as people had obviously seen the ambulance come and go. Noel said that Mum knew the moment she got out of her car and saw him waiting in the yard.

He'd tried to ring my phone, but I'd had it on silent, which is why he'd rung Nicole. Mum couldn't talk to me because she was too upset, and I finished by telling him I'd be there as soon as I could.

'I've got to get over there now,' I said to Nicole. I was numb. I couldn't believe he was dead. My Dad was my hero. I'd idolised him all my life. He'd been invincible on the football field and had carried that aura off it, yet somehow he was gone at just fifty-one. I couldn't work it out. 'Why?' I kept saying as I buried my head in my hands.

Just a couple of months earlier we were having the time of our lives celebrating the Grand Final victory. He had been so proud of my achievement, and some of those moments spent with him reflecting on the victory were the best of my life. And it was only just over three weeks before that he'd driven me to the airport to send me back out to Australia to try and win another Premiership. I was in shock and didn't know what to do. For the first time I realised how far away I really was from my family.

Fucking Australia. Why is it so far away?

I was glad when Elaine O'Gorman, a familiar face from back home, arrived on the doorstep. She and her husband Oliver had been great friends to me during my time in Sydney, and she'd almost been like a second mother to me. They were first cousins of Noel's fiancée Isabelle, and she'd obviously been told about what had happened and had come straight over, even though it was the middle of the night.

All I could think about was getting home, so I rang Andrew Ireland. 'Andrew, my old man has died,' I said before bursting into tears again and passing the phone to Nicole.

It turned out that I couldn't get on a plane until 5 p.m., which made me angrier and angrier. Elaine tried to keep me busy. She got me out of the house for breakfast and took me to the hairdresser's. Doyley was also doing everything he could, and we were both still spooked by the fire alarm. We'd figured out that it had gone off at roughly the time Dad had died. It was freaky and we still couldn't come up with an explanation for how it had worked when we were both convinced it had been disconnected months before.

Outjumping Brent Harvey of the Kangaroos during the match on 2 April 2005 in Canberra.

My famous jig during the presentation of my AFL medal on 24 September 2005, a salute to my Irish fans. I was almost better known for this than for winning the medal!

Mum, Dad and uncle Mikey in the stand at Melbourne during the Premiership final in 2005.

My biggest inspiration. It was so special to have Dad there immediately after winning. This was a very emotional and memorable moment.

Me with Swans' assistant coach and my mentor George Stone.

I always enjoyed the craic with the Swans' fans. This was the day after the big win when they held a reception for us at the SCG.

Down to business. Getting instructions from Jack O'Connor before the league match against Derry in spring 2009. Jack and I had a close bond from my time with the Under-21s. This was my first run-out with Kerry and a bit of a change from Sydney!
© Oliver McVeigh/SPORTSFILE

The Munster championship against Cork. A disappointing defeat which strengthened our resolve. This was the start of the long road to Croker.

Paul Galvin and myself developed a great on-field understanding. Here we are just before kick-off in the All-Ireland semi-final. I was named man of the match that day. It was a tough day at the office.

A dream come true. Holding aloft the Sam Maguire after winning the All-Ireland final on 20 September 2009.

© David Maher/SPORTSFILE

Nicole was going to come over with me to Listowel, and the club had also arranged for George Stone to be with us. I was like a zombie. I was functioning, but my mind was elsewhere. I took four sleeping tablets on the plane, but even they didn't work. I then began one of the hardest things I've ever done. I started writing a speech for my father's funeral.

Because I wasn't at home there was still a part of me that was hanging onto the belief that it wasn't really true. I hadn't been there. I hadn't seen it or experienced anything to do with it, because I'd been so far away. It didn't take long for that to be stripped away, and the moment I saw my uncle Mikey and our next-door neighbour Brian O'Brien waiting for us at the airport, it started to become real. Dad had always been the one who picked me up at the airport.

Not much was said on the trip to Listowel, as there really wasn't much to say. I stared blankly out of the window for most of the journey, but as soon as we pulled up outside the house my stomach started to churn. There were cars everywhere and when I got to the gate I froze.

'I don't want to go in,' I said. 'I don't want to go in.'

I knew that when I went inside it would become real. My Dad would be gone. I knew that his body was lying in an open casket, so for the past two days there would have been people calling in non-stop to pay their respects. I had to be almost pushed in the door. When I saw Mum, Joanne and Noel I broke down again. We hugged each other, and Mum whispered to us, 'Just stick close together. Stay close together for each other.'

'We loved you, Dad.'

Noel's words rung out through St Mary's church. I was standing alongside him at the dais facing the hundreds of mourners who had crammed inside to honour our father.

'To many, he was known as the great Tim Kennelly, the legend and "the Horse", but to Mum he was a husband and best friend. They loved each other very much,' Noel said. 'To Tadhg, Joanne and me he was the best Dad ever. He inspired us, touched us and helped us. So many people in their everyday lives experienced this as well. He was fair and honest and hard, but he was a great family man.'

It was my turn next, and I had to take several deep breaths to gather myself. I'd decided to tell a few funny stories about the man we all loved. I explained that he'd tried many things in his life, including horse training and greyhound racing, and that he had taken part in politics, canvassing with his friend and former teammate Jimmy Deenihan, a Fine Gael TD for Kerry North.

'So here we are on a Saturday afternoon,' I said. 'It's a full house, Timmy, a beautiful Saturday afternoon, and I think there are more All-Ireland medals than people here, so I thank everyone for coming.

'Growing up on the football field, there were a few things he always tried to instil in Noel and me as footballers. One was if we made a few sprints and a few efforts and were a bit tired, the first thing we did as young fellas was put our hands on our hips. Then you would always hear, without fail, "Take your hands off your hips." He believed it showed a sign of weakness to your opponent, that you were tired, and I think to this day Noel and I have never put our hands on our hips on a football field.

'And the second was that if your opponents were giving you a bit of hard time and a bit of attention, again without fail, and it's as vivid as if he was here right now, he'd say, "God didn't give you elbows to pick your nose so use them boy."' Laughter broke out in the church followed by a round of applause. Everyone there could picture Tim Kennelly uttering those words.

'Now, I'd like to just take a moment for everyone to remember some time that he inspired and touched you,' I said, but by then my voice was breaking. 'He made you laugh, and I think he was a Dad to a lot of people around here, so just take a moment ...' I couldn't finish the sentence.

The support our family had received over the previous few days had been overwhelming. My hand was actually bruised from shaking it so much – it was literally black and blue – and my back was sore from the constant embraces. People came from all over the country, with my Dad's teammates from the great Kerry era there en masse. It was a major shock for them, because he was the first to go, the first member of arguably the greatest team of all time to pass away. Many of his opponents, including Dublin star Tony Hanahoe, with whom Dad had many legendary battles, were also in the church, along with representatives of the GAA and many county boards. Former Ireland rugby international Moss Keane was also there.

Dad's death had led the national TV news and been on the front page of every Irish paper. There was a minute's silence in parliament in honour of him, and the president, Mary McAleese, sent a letter with her condolences, while the Taoiseach sent an aide to represent the government at the funeral. All through the streets of Listowel people had put up photos of Dad, with the green and gold of Kerry and the black and gold of the Emmets decorating the town.

The jerseys of his two teams were laid on the coffin, which was led by a lone piper through the town to John Paul II cemetery on the Ballybunion Road. Thousands of people formed a guard of honour along the street and it was one of the most moving experiences of my life. I thought I was going to lose it a number of times as we began the slow walk, my head leaning into the wooden casket. Noel was on the opposite side, and there were six of us carrying the coffin, including Dad's two brothers, his old manager Mick O'Dwyer and teammate Jack O'Shea. About halfway to the cemetery someone said, 'Fucking hell. How heavy is he?'

It broke the ice, and we managed to have a little laugh together. Then O'Shea, who was one of the greatest players in Kerry history, summed it up perfectly. 'Well, there is a horse in there.'

At the cemetery there was another brief ceremony, with a huge crowd gathering at the new graveyard. Billy Keane, the son of John B. Keane, a sports writer and author, introduced two of Dad's closest friends for the final tributes – Jimmy

Deenihan, who'd played alongside Dad in all of his five All-Ireland victories, and Stephen Slack, a local player with Listowel who'd also played for Kerry.

Slack recalled an image of Dad that had remained with him. 'I was sixteen years of age, and it was January. He was wintering well after an All-Ireland, and he was carrying, as Mick O'Dwyer used to say, a little bit of condition. I knew that was the case, because it was unusual to see a man wearing two tracksuits and a black polythene sack. I saw at first hand the kind of punishment the man was prepared to put his body through to achieve his sporting goals.'

He then recalled his last conversation with Dad, following the Emmets' victory over Finuge in the north Kerry semi-final the previous Sunday. 'I asked him, "How are we going to beat Ballyduff in the final?" We spoke for about an hour, and I can actually feel him looking down at me now and saying, "Stephen, say no more in case there's a few of 'em listening."'

Deenihan spoke about the bond that the great Kerry team had and how proud he was to see them all there to say goodbye to their favourite son. 'There was a great bond between our team on the field of play,' he said. 'I felt that special bond outside the church today and in the church last night. There was a special bond – something that people would not understand unless they played on that team. There was a special understanding. Words didn't have to be said. People understood each other. It just came spontaneously to us. It was intuitive. It was within us.'

He then explained that Tim Kennelly had always been the man to lift the team when the pressure was at its greatest. 'Football was his life,' Deenihan said. 'He was a total football fanatic. Off the field he was a gentleman, the kind of man who was always seen but not heard.'

After the ceremony ended and the crowd started slowly to disperse Jack O'Shea, a man who I idolised and revered, came up and looked me straight in the eye and said something that I would never forget. 'You know what you have to do.'

Chapter 14

A week after Dad's funeral Noel and I ran out for Listowel in the local championship final. I knew I'd told Sydney I would never play for my old club again, but there was no way I was missing this game. In hindsight neither of us should have played. I was still an emotional wreck, and as much as I tried to focus on getting the ball and kicking goals my heart wasn't in it. We lost the game, and it actually just confused me even more.

Jack O'Shea's words were still haunting me. I knew exactly what he meant. I knew my father's wish was for me to one day come back to Ireland and win an All-Ireland medal with Kerry. I just didn't know if I was ready to do it then. I was confused, and my only escape was drinking. I felt like if I drank, the pain would go away, so I kept doing it and doing it.

The Swans had been really supportive of my situation and had sent a card from all the players with small messages from each one written on it. They'd also had a minute's silence at training in honour of the passing of my father. But they were the farthest thing from my mind at that moment. I had gone from an unbelievable high to such a devastating low in a short period of time, and it had rocked me to the core.

I started to develop a real hatred for Australia, because I felt as though it had robbed me of the chance to get to know my father. The age of eighteen to twenty-four are the years when you really learn about who you are and about the people closest to you. It was then that I should have got to hear all the stories of what Dad had done and what he was like. But I felt I didn't get that chance, that Australia had taken me away from him. I hated the place and I didn't want to go back. Over and over in my mind I kept telling myself I should never have gone. I should never have left my father.

I visited his grave every day for the next five weeks. A couple of times I attempted to do some training, heading down to the beach at Ballybunion to try and get myself out of the black hole I was falling into. It's a spectacular area down there, famous for its beautiful golf course, which is regarded as one of the best in the world. There is a statue of former US president Bill Clinton there because it's one of his favourite courses, and all the superstars of golf, including Tiger Woods, have walked the fairways of the amazing links course. Several holes run along the edge of the cliffs, and it was at the bottom of these that I would train when the tide was out. I would run along the sand and it could be extremely tough, with a strong sea breeze often knocking me around.

The Swans had sent over a training programme, but I found that I'd complete maybe one sprint and then just pack it in. 'What the fuck is the point?' I asked myself as I was being almost blown over by the wind.

Twice I'd tentatively booked flights back to Sydney, and both times I'd cancelled them. Each time I'd rung Roosy and simply said, 'I'm not ready.' The latest plan had me flying to Los Angeles on 15 January to meet the Swans, who were playing an exhibition match against the Kangaroos as part of the Australia Week celebrations. I'd spoken a lot to George about my struggles, but it was really Mum who eventually got me moving, almost pushing me out the door. She could see that I was losing my way, that I was feeling sorry for myself and that it was only going to get worse if I stayed in Listowel. Mum sensed that I thought I still had some unfinished business in the AFL, and Noel joined her in convincing me to go back, for the short term at least.

'Go back, and if you don't settle, you can always come back,' Noel said. 'We just don't want you looking back in four or five years and saying that you might have made a mistake. We don't want you to have any regrets.'

It was arranged that Nicole would fly to Ireland and then join me on the trip to LA. I was still very confused when Mum and Noel drove me to the airport. I had experienced some excruciating emotions over the previous six weeks, but getting out of the car and saying goodbye to my mother topped the lot. 'I don't want to go,' I said as I cried in her arms.

I was abandoning her when she needed me the most. Just like I hadn't been there for my father, I was now walking away from my mother. The tears turned to anger by the time I got to the terminal, and I seriously felt like I could kill someone. My mood hadn't improved much by the time I reached LA and caught up with the boys. It was a difficult time, because they were very much in party mode given that the trip to the US was getting them away from the grind of pre-season and giving them the opportunity to get on the drink for a week. I just couldn't do it.

I wasn't much fun to be around, but I was hopeful that getting back into a routine in Sydney might change things. Things were at least ticking over before a brief second of madness thrust me unexpectedly back into the spotlight.

Each year every AFL club had to participate in a community camp during the pre-season, which was all about the players getting out into the country and promoting the game. This time around the Swans were doing the rounds in Wollongong, which was on the south coast about two hours from Sydney. School visits are always the most important part of the camps, and I lucked out, doing a Catholic girls' school with Schneids and Lewis Roberts-Thompson. Everything was going fine until LRT was asked by a student what his most embarrassing moment was. He paused and was struggling to come up with one, so I crept up behind him and pulled his shorts down and said, 'This is.'

I knew he was wearing Speedos, as we'd just completed a swimming session, so there wasn't any danger of anything inappropriate popping out. The students erupted in laughter, and I was having a good chuckle myself, although the teachers didn't seem to share our humour. Little did I know that a photographer had captured the whole thing, and by the next morning it was all over the papers, with the incident becoming a massive talking point. Talk radio debated whether Australia had become too politically correct given the outrage that had followed the 'dacking' incident. I had never heard the word 'dacking', which is very much an Australian term. The reaction was absurdly out of proportion, and it even made it onto the front page of a paper back in Ireland.

The club had to go into damage control, so the next day I was back at the school with Roosy to apologise. First we had to go into the principal's office, then I was going to speak to the students. I figured I would apologise for my 'brain snap', and the whole thing would disappear, but the principal started lecturing me and questioning my faith. I flipped out, because there was no way anyone was going to question my religious beliefs, given what I had just gone through with the passing of my father. Thankfully, Roosy calmed things down.

When I got to the hall to issue my apology it wasn't just the students who'd been present at the infamous dacking but the whole school that was present. I told them I was sorry and that it was irresponsible for me to have done such a thing. I couldn't believe how big the whole thing had become. I did laugh, though, as I left, when some of the girls came up to me and said how much they loved it and that it was the funniest thing they'd seen. It was certainly political correctness gone mad, but I learned a valuable lesson: no more dacking on community camps for me!

Getting back to training turned out to be best thing for me. It gave me something to focus on, a distraction from the emptiness I was carrying around. I also tried some retail therapy by buying my dream car, a Holden Monaro. But just when I thought I was finding my feet again, another curve ball was sent my way. This time it was in the form of a serious shoulder injury. We were playing an intra-club practice match, and I was in a contest with first-year player Ryan Brabazon, when he edged me out. Unfortunately, while my body was moving forward my left shoulder was going backwards, and I felt it pop straight out. It seemed to go back in a few seconds later, and when Roosy came over I told him I thought I'd be right for our first proper practice match of the season the following week against Essendon at the North Sydney Oval.

I'd actually given the same shoulder a knock in Ireland when I'd had a tumble while out on the drink, but everything had seemed fine when I'd gone for a precautionary scan the next day. That wasn't how the specialist in Sydney saw things and he informed me that I required a full shoulder reconstruction. According to Gibbsy this normally meant at least a twelve-to-sixteen-week recovery period. But there was no way after all I'd been through that I was going to sit on my arse and kiss half the season goodbye because of a silly shoulder injury. Like I had done with my knee injury a couple of years earlier, I became obsessed about getting back in half the time. Gibbsy tried to caution me about pushing it too hard, but there was no way I was going to hold back. Pain wasn't an issue.

This isn't pain. Losing my old man was fucking pain.

I knew I had changed as a person since Dad had died. I was still very angry, and I was selfish, focusing entirely on myself and nothing else. That made me extremely hard to deal with for my teammates and people at the club. It was almost like they didn't know what to say to me, and I often felt people were dodging around the issue and not really attempting to understand what I was going through.

I was lonely. There were many times in bed late at night when I bawled my eyes out, my thoughts inevitably drifting to my father. What I missed most of all was my family, to be able to talk to them, to ask Mum how she was feeling. I wasn't there for them again. Nicole tried to help, but I just ended up pushing her away. She suffered because she represented Australia, and I was still very, very angry with what I thought the country had done to me. It was unfair, but I was looking for people to blame.

In many ways I'd gone full circle. Whereas initially I had struggled to find my comfort zone on the field, now it was all I had. Training or playing was the only time I could escape from my pain, which is why I became fanatical about the rehabilitation of my shoulder. After just three weeks I was making noises about being ready for round one because I was able to move the arm. This notion was ridiculous, but it showed how determined I was to get back. However, it turned out to be a good game to miss, given we opened our Premiership defence in 2006 by conceding nine goals to Essendon in the first quarter at Telstra Dome. In the end the margin was twenty-seven points and it was certainly not the performance of a reigning Premier. Things didn't improve the following week, despite the unfurling of the Premiership flag in a ceremony before our first home game of the season, against Port Adelaide. It was strange for me to watch it, because sadly I would always remember 2005 as the year my father died and not the year I won a Premiership Medal in Australia.

The hype and build-up didn't help our cause, with another loss, this time by twenty-six points. We finally got on the winner's list the following week, but it was in less than spectacular style, grinding out a seven-point win against the previous year's wooden-spooners Carlton at Telstra Dome.

Watching us struggle so badly had given me even more reason to push hard for selection, and this time Gibbsy and Roosy were more welcoming. I passed all the tests from the medical side of things, and my coach knew me well enough that he trusted my judgement about whether I was ready or not. This meant that I had made a complete mockery of medical science according to Gibbsy by returning from shoulder reconstruction in six weeks, halving the normal recovery period.

Roosy asked whether I wanted to start on the ground – we were playing Melbourne at the SCG – but I thought it would be good to start on the bench and then get the crowd involved when I came on, which might help get the boys going. It might also help calm me down, because I knew I would be very emotional given that it was my first game since Dad had died.

I wanted to ensure he would be with me all the time. A couple of months after I returned to Sydney I had the word

'Father' tattooed down the left-hand side of my torso. It was on that side because it was close to my heart, and Noel got the same tattoo. Doyley helped me investigate the traditional style of lettering I wanted and was with me at the Surry Hills tattoo parlour when I went through a couple of hours of absolute agony. It was so painful because there was hardly any fat in that area of my body.

I also got my boot sponsor Puma to put *Athair* – the Gaelic word for father – on the tongue of my boots. I knew if anyone else saw it, they wouldn't know what it meant. It was my own little motivational tool. I knew I would only have to look down at it during a game and it would get me going. I also wore a black armband, and I was so narrow in my focus everything was about, 'Doing it for Dad.'

He was all I was thinking about as I ran onto the SCG field to the massive roar of the crowd. Even though the play was down the other end, Melbourne captain David Neitz ran straight into me. I had deliberately worn a long-sleeved jumper, so it wasn't obvious which was the problem shoulder.

'Wrong shoulder, you dickhead,' I said as I laughed in his face.

He had another go, but this time he didn't get very far because Leo Barry came out of nowhere and flattened him. I had no problem with the shoulder and managed to collect seventeen possessions, although we just came up short, losing by five points. Thankfully, things began to click after that, and we won six games on the trot to get our season rolling.

It wasn't long after my return that the media began to focus on my contract. It would run out at the end of the season and everyone was asking if I would be going home. The Swans understood my situation. They weren't putting any pressure on, and I really didn't know what to do, which is why I decided to fly Mum and Joanne out later in the year. While I talked to Mum almost every single day it wasn't the same as seeing her in person and really being able to understand her feelings.

My own feelings fluctuated throughout the year. There were some days when I would ring Roosy and say, 'I don't think I want to come in today.' Mentally, I was all over the shop, and I found my mind sometimes wandering to memories of my father during games, which began to affect my performances. I was finding it hard, because if you are struggling mentally, it is very difficult to attack the physical side of things with the required level of intensity.

It wasn't just me who seemed to have the blues. The team also had a midseason slump, losing four out of five, although one of those was yet another epic encounter with our arch-rivals West Coast at Subiaco in Perth in round fifteen. Once again it was a cracker of a game, and we should have won, given that we kicked six goals in the opening quarter. Unfortunately, we only managed three more for the game and went down by just two points, although we were on the short end of some questionable umpiring decisions. The game did show that although we had some ups and downs throughout the season, when it came to the big games and the big occasion this Swans team was as good as anyone in the competition. We then went on to win six of the last seven games of the regular season to book our spot in the September action.

In the lead-up to the final home-and-away game I announced that I would be re-signing for another three years. The decision had been the hardest of my life, and I only reached it after spending three weeks discussing every detail with my mother. In the end I did the same thing that I did when I made the decision to come to Australia when I was seventeen. I got a piece of paper, put a line down the middle and wrote down the pros and cons of staying.

A big factor was my sense of unfinished business. I thought at twenty-five I was just coming into the best years of my career, and so were the Swans. I figured our Premiership window was still open for another two or three years. Also, it made sense financially to stay, as it would give me an opportunity to set up my whole family.

I knew Mum's preferred option was for me to come home, although she never said so in as many words. I also knew that everyone back in Listowel was convinced I would come home. But when I explained to Mum that I intended to move back to Ireland once my new AFL contract was up she started to come round.

'Family is always first with me, and that is what has made this decision even harder. The fact is that I still want to stay, because I think I'm not ready to go back,' I told a packed media conference in the club's boardroom, the 2005 Premiership

Cup sitting proudly behind me in a glass case. 'It's hard trying to please everyone. I know a lot of people at home are disappointed. But it has made it easier knowing that there is a three-year deadline. That has made it easier for my Mum … and the fact that I have said that I am going to live in Ireland. That is where I am going to bring up my kids. That is where I want to have a family, not here in Australia.'

One of the key negotiating points had been the Swans giving me permission to have a three- to four-month break at the end of each season at home in Ireland. This was very much driven by Roosy, who understood the pull of home given that his wife Tammy was American and had gone through similar issues. I'd done seven pre-seasons, so he knew I didn't need an extensive pre-Christmas training block, and he trusted me to show up in January in reasonable shape.

Roosy couldn't help but try to keep the door ajar at the end of the press conference. 'I guess I've got three years to talk him into staying,' he quipped.

It was a big relief to have finally made the decision, because I needed a clear head given what confronted us in the opening week of the finals – another date with West Coast at Subiaco. They'd finished on top with a 17–5 record, and we'd snuck into fourth spot on percentage which was an important part of the make-up of the AFL ladder. The percentage of each team was calculated by having the total points scored by a team throughout the season divided by the points scored against it and multiplied by 100. But statistics and percentages meant nothing when it came to West Coast–Sydney clashes and once again this one was an epic.

The game followed a similar pattern to the round fifteen clash, as we started brilliantly, kicking seven goals to four in the first half to lead by fifteen points. Hally and Mickey O were looking dangerous up front, Goodesy was running with West Coast's superstar captain Chris Judd and holding up his end of the bargain, Kirky was at the bottom of every pack, while Leo and I were providing plenty of rebound from defence. Then, as expected, the Eagles surged, cutting our lead to just three points at three-quarter time.

In keeping with tradition the last quarter was another enthralling, tight contest. The pressure was extreme, and it came down to which team could hold their nerve. Because we'd done it so many times in recent years I was confident that the Bloods would find a way, but I also knew that I was almost out on my feet. The Eagles' three big guns – Judd, Ben Cousins and Dean Cox – had all lifted their games in the final quarter, and with the clock ticking past twenty-five minutes they led by five points. Something had to happen and fast. The ball was in their forward pocket when Luke Ablett gathered and fed off a quick handball to Amon Buchanan, who sensed the urgency of the situation. Throughout his career Monty had showed a knack for getting out of tight situations, and this time he managed to wriggle out of a tackle and handball it to me. I had a quick look inside, but there was a better option out near the boundary line, and my twenty-five-metre pass hit Davo on the chest.

The good thing about the passage of play was that not only were we out of the danger area, but that we had players running through the middle of the ground. Davo handballed over the top to Goodesy, who did the same thing, putting the ball out in front of Nic Fosdike, who flicked off a handball to Nick Malceski, a talented young left-footer who was playing in his first final. He was a beautiful kicker, but his attempt to get the ball to Ryan O'Keefe wasn't a good one, and it dropped short, which allowed Eagles defender Drew Banfield to punch it away. However, his spoil travelled twenty metres towards our goal, where Mickey O and his opponent, Brett Jones, were standing. In a stroke of fortune the ball bounced over the top of them, which opened the door for Mickey O to run onto it in the goal square and slam through the match-winner.

In his excitement Mickey O kept running up to the fence and roaring in the faces of the Eagles fans. He was just inches away from them and it was a priceless moment. While it wasn't quite Leo taking a mark to win the Premiership, the way the team had engineered the goal in the dying minutes, taking it from one end to the other, had put us in prime position to win back-to-back Premierships. When the siren sounded a minute or so later the scoreboard read 13.7 (85) to 12.12 (84). It was Sydney's first win at Subiaco since 2001 and the fourth consecutive match between the two teams that had been decided by four points or less.

It had certainly been another extraordinary game, and I was physically and mentally exhausted. The boys were pumped, but it was strange because although we were making a bit of noise celebrating the rest of the stadium had fallen deathly quiet. There were 40,000 people packed into the Subiaco Oval, but it felt as though we were at training with no one else there. The silence was incredible, but we well and truly broke it when we entered the changing-room. The win meant we had the week off and would play the preliminary final on our own turf at Telstra Stadium.

Twelve months earlier I'd left Perth thinking we'd blown the Premiership; this time I was convinced we'd just won it again. The loss must have cut deep with the Eagles, and I'm sure they were wondering if they were ever going to beat us in a close game that mattered. Our confidence was sky high, and when we arrived back in Sydney we hit the town, knowing we had plenty of time to recover.

This relaxed attitude stayed with us for the next week or so as we prepared for the preliminary final, which was against the other Western Australian team, Fremantle. They were a young and improving side who had finished in the top four for the first time since the club had entered the AFL in 1995. They'd had a fairy-tale season, but we were never going to give them a happy ending. Hally kicked six, and Mickey O and O'Keefe got four each as we had the game pretty much under control from the start, with the eventual margin of victory a comfortable thirty-five points.

Things could not have been more different compared with the previous year. The excitement and anxiousness of the unknown wasn't there, replaced instead by an air of expectation and a business-like approach. We were no longer the underdogs; we were the reigning champions who everyone expected to turn up to the MCG and deliver again on the last Saturday in September. And in a twist we would be playing our arch-enemy the Eagles again after they'd upset Adelaide on their home turf in the other preliminary final.

The week started on a good note for the Swans, with Goodesy winning his second Brownlow Medal. This time he won it outright, as back in 2003 he'd shared it with Collingwood captain Nathan Buckley and Adelaide star Mark Ricciuto.

My own preparation wasn't as hectic, given I was a bit more organised in dealing with the arrival of the Kennelly contingent. Noel didn't come out this time, with Mum joined by a handful of first and second cousins. While it was great to have them all there I couldn't help but think about the person who wasn't there – Dad.

One very positive difference this time around was the inclusion of my housemate Doyley in the Grand Final selection. Injuries had jinxed him for a number of years, but this time he was up and running and the perfect replacement for Jason Ball, who had retired after previous year's win, as had fellow veteran Paul Williams. There were three other new faces in the team: former Essendon player Ted Richards, young midfielder Jarrad McVeigh and Nick Malceski.

While the Grand Final parade was as spectacular as the previous year, it didn't have the same buzz about it for me, as it was no longer new. The whole build-up didn't really have any zing, which I hoped was a good sign, illustrating that we were calm and in control.

The morning of the game was also very different, as my morning's TV viewing had been ruined because there was no Channel Ten crew in Listowel that year. An Irishman winning his second Premiership Medal clearly wasn't as newsworthy as him winning his first.

I had learned a few lessons from the previous year in terms of my pre-game preparation and was nowhere near as nervous. Everything was familiar, and we stuck to the same routine that had been successful twelve months earlier. Things that had blown my mind the first time around, such as running out onto the field, the noise, the crowd, the tension as the national anthem was sung, were no longer a big deal.

The first sign of tension came the moment I saw my opponent walking towards me.

Fucking taggers.

Rowan Jones had missed the previous year's Grand Final because of injury, but I had crossed paths with him a few times, and his sole focus had always been to shut me down. Taggers were players who had no interest in getting the ball themselves, they were only worried about negating their opponent. I knew Jones couldn't do me for pace, but the problem was he would just keep running all day, which meant I had to keep following him.

Man, this is going to be a long day.

I was right, because for the opening five minutes the ball didn't go anywhere near me, and when I had my first opportunity to get a possession I slipped and fell on my arse. And my teammates weren't going much better. We weren't switched on, and suddenly it felt as though we'd taken the laid-back, relaxed build-up a bit too far. The Eagles were hungry, and we should have been prepared for that, but it was obvious we weren't.

In the opening ten minutes West Coast kicked three goals to one behind. We were making uncharacteristic errors, fumbling the ball when we normally wouldn't, and our skills were off. It wasn't until Mickey O marked on the lead and slotted the shot that we had our first goal. I started to get involved and had a major confidence boost when I got the better of Cousins in a crucial one-on-one contest on the wing. I 'soccered' the ball off the ground and then managed to edge him off its line as we sprinted after it, which enabled me to pick it up, take a bounce and kick long to Luke Ablett, who, in keeping with how badly we were doing, dropped the mark.

At quarter-time I was the Swans' leading possession winner with six, but we were behind by sixteen points and struggling big time. There was no panic in the huddle, but we needed to get ourselves into the game as soon as possible. At that stage the Eagles had touched the ball sixty more times than us, which said a lot. Not a lot changed in the first ten minutes of the second quarter, and when Eagles full-forward Quinten Lynch kicked two goals in as many minutes the lead was out to twenty-eight points. Mickey O got one back for us before I found myself under the spotlight.

After chipping to the back pocket from the kick-out I got the ball back just outside the goal square, and with no options forthcoming I thought I needed to make something happen. All I had to do was get around Cousins. This was no problem, as 'selling the dummy' was the one Aussie rules skill that I'd been a master of from day one, thanks to my Gaelic football background. As I shaped to kick, Cousins was exactly where I wanted him, as he'd transferred his weight to one side and was probably going to attempt to smother the ball.

Oh shit. What just happened?

I was on the ground. I had slipped *again* on the turf.

Quick. Get rid of it.

I put the ball down on the ground with one hand as I landed. I then swung my arm to hit it away, but by that stage Cousins had grabbed hold of my jumper. I thought I'd got away with it, as the ball was rolling towards a couple of my teammates, when I heard the whistle.

Noooooooooooooo!

'Dropping the ball,' I heard the umpire say as he raced in. I couldn't believe that something that I'd done a hundred times before had just gone horribly wrong. It got even worse as I watched Cousins kick the goal from thirty metres. Jones and a couple of West Coast players then tried to get in my face, but my teammates pushed them away. That moment pretty much summed up the first half for all of us, although a late goal from

Davo at least reduced the margin to twenty-five points at the main break.

From the moment we stepped into the changing-room I was away. 'I don't give a fuck who is playing shit,' I screamed as I paced the room. 'Don't be fucking sorry for yourself. Pull your heads out of your arse. We've got another half to play in a Grand Final. There is plenty of fucking time.'

I was going nuts, as was Kirky, who was our captain for the day. We'd become extremely close over the year, as we both very much played from the heart. In many ways I'd become the emotional centre of the team in 2006, because the players could see how much I was hurting after the loss of my father and how driven I was to succeed. My problem was that I struggled to understand that not everyone had the same passion to win as I had and that people reacted in different ways to defeat. After a loss I would feel as if my heart had been ripped out of my chest, but others would seem to take it in their stride, often laughing in the changing-room just minutes afterwards, which drove me mad. 'They don't give a fuck about the club. They should be trying harder to win,' I would constantly say to Kirky. 'They just don't give a fuck.'

For a long time I expected everyone to play as though their lives depended on it, and it took me a long time to realise that not everyone approached the game like that. Kirky did, which was why we had a special bond, one which had become so close that the boys had started to joke that we were in a relationship.

I would say anything to anyone if they weren't performing on the field. I'd always been that way from the day I started, and I was getting into the faces of my teammates now. I found that by speaking up and energising people, it actually fired me up because I knew I couldn't come out and say all this stuff and then not back it up on the field. The problem was that a lot of players who were having a down day would go into a cocoon, not say anything and just worry about their own patch. That was the last thing we needed to happen. If we were going to get back into this game, it had to be an across-the-board effort as a team.

Ninety seconds into the third quarter we scored a goal. Schneids made a brilliant run-down from behind to win a free kick, but the advantage rule allowed Hally, who'd been well held in the first half, to handball over the top to Mickey O, who kicked his third goal. There wasn't another goal kicked for fifteen minutes, as the traditional struggle between the two teams went to an even higher level. Unfortunately, it was the Eagles and Andrew Embley who broke the drought, but Davo answered back a couple of minutes later.

Even though we were clearly playing better, the margin was still twenty-five points midway through the quarter when Lynch goaled from a tight set-shot in the pocket. That had been a problem all day: we'd missed fairly easy shots while the Eagles had nailed everything. The unlikely figure of defender Lewis Roberts-Thompson got the scoreboard moving the right way again after Goodesy released him with a good handball.

Despite being tackled, his kick just managed to sail over the heads of players in the goal square.

Kirky then hit the post and Hally missed a sitter from twenty-five metres out directly in front. We were now dominating play but needed to put more pressure on the scoreboard. It was Grand Final debutant Richards, who'd been excellent in defence all day, who set up Davis with a great pass in the final minute of the third quarter. The enigmatic Davo was certainly on form and another beautiful shot at goal meant the margin had been reduced to eleven points at three-quarter time.

There wasn't any need for yelling and screaming at the last break. You could sense the confidence rising in the group, because we knew how good our track record was in these tight situations. We would just strangle and strangle the Eagles until they wilted. Everyone in that huddle knew we'd find a way to win, because that's what the Bloods did, and it's what we'd done twelve months earlier.

Fourteen seconds into the final quarter we were rolling. Doyley tapped the ball from a centre square bounce-down to McVeigh, whose quick kick found Hally at centre half-forward. He immediately shot out a handball to Goodesy, who nailed the goal on the run from fifty-five metres.

Here we come. We're going to do it again.

Incredibly, there were no goals scored for the next fifteen minutes. Both defences were under siege, and I was forced to rush a behind at one stage, which wasn't ideal given that the game was set to be decided by less than a goal. Nothing was happening for us offensively until Schneids pulled a rabbit out of his hat. It was a bread-and-butter move for a forward pocket, being front and centre at a marking contest, but it was his poise and finish on his non-preferred right foot that made it so brilliant. His goal put us just one point down with seven minutes remaining on the clock.

Thirty seconds later the Eagles replied in very similar fashion, with their own goalsneak, Steven Armstrong, reading the ball perfectly off the pack and then deliberately kicking the ball along the ground, bouncing it end over end and through the goal from twenty metres out. We went one better, because it only took us twenty seconds to manufacture a response. O'Keefe marked the ball on the boundary line fifty metres out and played on straight away, swinging onto his natural left foot and banging it towards the goal square. There were four players in the area, but somehow they all managed to miss it, and the ball bounced through for a goal.

Unbelievable. Surely, this shows it's meant to be.

Suddenly, every possession counted. There was no longer any room for error. One little mistake could cost us a Premiership, and one little stroke of brilliance could win it. Unfortunately, it was the Eagles who produced the latter, with regular defender Daniel Chick, who had just been moved forward, blocking a clearing kick from O'Keefe and then managing to pick up the loose ball and handball it over to his teammate Adam Hunter, who ran into an open goal. The margin was now seven points, and we needed two goals in five minutes to win.

We had to attack at all costs, and every possession was now banged hard and long into the forward line. Although the Eagles were getting numbers back we knew something would give, and it did. Monty Buchanan bounced out of a couple of tackles in the forward pocket and handballed out to Nick Malceski, who despite being in his first Grand Final, calmly turned onto his trusty left foot and drilled the goal. The clock read twenty-six minutes, so I figured we had about three minutes left to find another goal.

The Eagles were playing it smart though, bottling up the stoppages and giving us a dose of our own medicine. They were wiping time off the clock, and after two consecutive bounces on the wing I called for everyone to clear out and let the likes of Kirky weave his magic. It worked, but again our forward thrust was knocked out of bounds. The ball was at least on the half-forward line, and with the clock closing on thirty-one minutes I knew that this was almost certainly our last roll of the dice.

The ball was thrown back in, with Doyley and Cox going at it, when suddenly I stopped dead as if shot.

Oh my God. That's the siren. We've lost. We've fucking lost. What happened?

It felt like a sniper in the crowd had taken me out. My body had instantly been drained and all that was left was a massive empty feeling.

This isn't meant to happen. This isn't what happens to the Swans. We don't lose games by a point.

I slumped to the turf. Eventually, I got up, and we all came together in a group off to the side of the stage, with Roosy going to every player and congratulating them on their efforts. It had been a phenomenal performance, coming from almost five goals down to lose by only a point. But as I watched the Eagles celebrate my mind drifted back to twelve months earlier and how that had been me enjoying the greatest hour of my life.

I could sense myself getting more and more upset and then I realised I was crying. It had been the toughest year of my life. I had carried with me the hurt of my father passing and had channelled all my anger into achieving one goal – winning another Premiership Medal for him.

I'm sorry, Dad. I'm so sorry I've let you down.

CHAPTER 15

I was ashamed to be an AFL footballer.

Never before had I felt that way, but what I was watching from the sidelines at Croke Park was making me sick. The second test of the 2006 International Rules series had erupted, with fights breaking out all over the pitch. It seemed the Australians were going to the knuckle, sniping Irish players off the ball. For someone who had championed the AFL cause for the past six years I was embarrassed by what was happening in front of me. And very frustrated that I wasn't out there after having suffered an early knock in the ribs, ironically from my Sydney teammate Barry Hall.

Ireland had won the opening test match in Galway by eight points, but the build-up to this match had been heated, with the Australians declaring that they would target Graham Geraghty, who had been booked for kneeing Lindsay Gilbee. They had certainly kept their word, and when the Meath star was knocked out after being slung in a tackle by Danyle Pearce, I thought a riot was going to break out. Seán Boylan, our coach, was furious, and he approached his Australian counterpart, Essendon legend Kevin Sheedy, several times to express his anger. By quarter-time his rage was uncontrollable, and he told officials he was pulling his side out of the match. It was only after pleas from the players that he relented. Already three Australian and three Irish players had been issued yellow cards.

While I thought Geraghty's injury was genuinely an accident, caused by a legitimate tackle, the behaviour of some of the Australians was over the top. I had no problem with the likes of Hawthorn's Campbell Brown being physical, because that was the way he played back at home, but what I couldn't stomach was other players who weren't known for playing this way in Australia suddenly throwing their weight around. The sight of some players running around nailing people was making my blood boil.

The Australians didn't understand that Geraghty and Brendan Coulter, who was also taken to hospital with facial injuries, were expected to turn up to work the next day. Being amateurs meant that if one of the Irish players had their jaw broken and was forced to miss a month of work, he was out of pocket, which then impacted on his family and his way of life. Players in Australia are guaranteed payment whether they play or don't play, and the majority make their living solely from playing football.

A misunderstanding in the interpretation of the rules was at the root of the problems. I could see it from both sides. Some of the things that the Aussies thought were unacceptable were part of the Irish game, while the tackling side of the hybrid game was what continually got the Irish players fired up. They weren't used to being thrown to the ground or being held down, so they reacted. Plus the Australians were significantly physically stronger, as the Gaelic players didn't know what the inside of a gym looked like.

The other issue I had was with the games being referred to as test matches. The use of the term added far too much weight to what were really just exhibitions. Playing in a test for your country in any sport is huge and there is a sense of pride associated with the term. If Ireland lost a 'test' match, the GAA would say, 'Boys, we are going to do everything we can to win this.' And Australia would do the same. If the events had been promoted as exhibition matches, it would have taken a lot of heat out of the equation.

I had been made vice-captain of the Ireland team at a camp that had been held in Toulouse, France, just a couple of weeks after the AFL Grand Final. I'd been drinking non-stop since the heartbreaking loss and had a lot of shit going around in my head. I felt lost and was questioning a lot of things in my life, so it's fair to say I wasn't in the best state to be showing any leadership qualities. I was rooming with Kerry player Aidan O'Mahoney, who was also in party mode because Kerry had won another All-Ireland title. I told the coaches that I had a calf strain so I didn't have to do too much training and just hit the town. My heart wasn't really in the series, because I felt like I'd done my thing for the year. I'd given everything to Sydney winning the flag and really didn't have much left in the tank.

Part of the deal in being named vice-captain was that I

was guaranteed the honour of captaining my country for the following year's series. I liked the sound of that, although after witnessing the fallout from the second test, I wasn't sure if there was going to be another International Rules series. It had already been hanging by a thread, with the GAA outraged by an on-field incident during the previous year's series in Australia, when Brisbane's Chris Johnson had gone berserk, punching Irish players Phillip Jordan and Mattie Forde.

Our coach's comments after the game didn't augur well for the future. 'I played in the county for twenty years, have been in team management for twenty-three, and as far as I'm concerned what happened out there in the first quarter today is not acceptable in any code of sport,' Boylan said. 'It's not acceptable on the street.'

By December, it was off. The GAA had notified the AFL they no longer wanted to take part in the series in its current format. I wasn't surprised, but was hopeful that when things cooled down and some rules were addressed it would resume down the track.

After taking the whole of November off I started my own personal training programme, with the treadmill getting a workout because the good old Irish weather couldn't be trusted. Being at home and having finally had some time off, I felt that after almost a year of grieving I was starting to understand that life goes on. While everything I did was still dedicated to my father I think I was now able to look forward and, more importantly, make sure I made him proud.

Pushing myself in training had never been a problem. I had taught myself very early on at the Swans how to push my body to the extreme. I vomited at every pre-season training session during the first three years. It got to the point that if I didn't feel like I was about to vomit, it meant I wasn't pushing hard enough. All the symptoms of extreme exertion, such as being light-headed, having blocked ears and experiencing dizziness, were fairly regular occurrences during my crazy training phase.

I was my own harshest critic. If during a training drill I didn't run hard enough, did a poor kick or made a mistake, I'd make myself do ten push-ups. The whole reason for this manic approach was that I knew I wanted to be in the best physical condition for round one. If I wasn't, I'd be found out. I needed to be able to run the arse off my opponent or break the heart of taggers.

I kept reminding myself of these things as I sprinted along the beach at Ballybunion. If I felt myself starting to lose focus, all I had to do was think about how the boys back in Sydney would be getting the shit flogged out of them in training. Noel couldn't believe that after I'd trained with the Emmets, I'd then do an extra hour of running immediately afterwards.

It was all worthwhile because when I got back to Sydney in the first week of January I was seriously primed. I was the best I'd been mentally and physically for a couple of years, and it showed when the new season started, although there was a disturbing case of déjà vu in round one. The AFL always scheduled the two Grand Finalists from the previous year to open the new season, which meant West Coast were coming to town.

A lot had changed in six months. While we'd made a few headlines by signing controversial ruckman Peter 'Spida' Everitt, who'd played 252 games for St Kilda and Hawthorn, the Eagles had surpassed us by managing to find themselves embroiled in one of the biggest scandals in AFL history. Ben Cousins, their former captain and superstar midfielder who'd won the 2005 Brownlow Medal, had been stood down indefinitely by the Eagles after admitting to being a drug addict. He'd then flown to the USA to seek treatment for a substance-abuse problem.

The Swans hierarchy had a theory that all the off-field controversy might galvanise the reigning Premiers, and that was certainly the case, with the Eagles kicking six straight goals in the opening quarter. They kicked another four in the second quarter, while we could only manage four behinds. Their lead was thirty-six points at half-time.

We were traditionally slow starters to the new season – we hadn't won a match in the pre-season competition since Roosy had taken over – but this was terrible. It certainly woke us up, and we slowly started to gain control of the match in the third quarter, kicking three goals and keeping the Eagles to just four behinds. The final quarter was your typical Sydney–West Coast arm-wrestle. Chris Judd and Daniel Kerr were fantastic for them, and with five minutes to go the margin was still nineteen points. That didn't matter to us, and we kicked three goals in as many minutes to give ourselves a chance to win it with one minute remaining on the clock. It looked like we would when Jarrad McVeigh found space at half-forward, but a brilliant diving tackle from Kerr stopped him from shooting for goal. We didn't get another chance, which meant, in an AFL first, the previous three games between Sydney and West Coast had all been decided by just one point.

Although I was naturally shattered to have lost another epic against the Eagles, I'd played well, finishing with twenty-six possessions. That was important because it proved once again that the harder you work, the better you play. Over the next three weeks I played some of the best football of my career, producing three twenty-plus possession games. I was flying. Enter Byron Pickett.

In round five we were playing Melbourne at the SCG. Once again I was finding plenty of ball, and in one particular play I took a mark at half-back and immediately played on. When I looked up there was no one forward, as Hally had led and was now doubling back. I knew I didn't have the legs to kick it far enough to reach him. Instead, I saw Melbourne's Pickett in front of me and figured I'd sell a dummy and get past him. I almost pulled it off, but he managed to latch onto my jumper. I stood up in the tackle and handballed as far as I could, but I'd twisted around. This meant that when he threw me to the ground my leg became caught and straight away I felt my right kneecap pop out.

What the fuck? What do I do?

I stared down at my knee and instinctively started whacking it to try and get the kneecap to go back into place so the pain would stop.

C'mon, you bastard. Go back in.

It wasn't happening. Finally, a couple of trainers and Gibbsy got to me, straightened my leg and clicked the kneecap back in.

How fucking easy was that? Why didn't I do that?

The problem was I couldn't walk on it, and I spent the rest of the afternoon watching from the bench with a massive bag of ice around my knee. I knew that I was looking at a fair stint on the sidelines, which is what Gibbsy confirmed after looking at scans of my knee. I had a grade-three medial tear as well as the knee dislocation. If I had the full operation, I could kiss the season goodbye; if I just had the medial repaired, it was a six-to-eight week recovery. I chose the latter, but made the call very early that I would be halving the time out.

Once again I clicked into obsession mode. To me it was very simple: I was here to play. I had given up so much to play this game that there was no use me sitting on the sidelines watching. I had shown in the past I was a super quick healer, so I went to work again. Everything, and I mean everything, revolved around getting my knee right. For two-and-a-half days I hardly slept, because I constantly had to keep ice on my injury. The quicker the swelling went down, something the ice accelerated, the better chance I had. I just pushed and pushed and pushed, and I became even more motivated as I watched the boys lose the next two games.

By the end of the second week I was back running, so I immediately declared I was going to play the following weekend against Port Adelaide. I increased the amount of running I was doing over the next few days, and then on the Wednesday before the game I stepped it up and sprinted flat out, with lots of turning and twisting as well. It was enough to at least get named in the team on Thursday, but I still had to get through training the next day.

I managed to do that, but I was in trouble when I woke up the following day. My knee was a bit sore, and I was shitting myself when I went around to Gibbsy's house in the afternoon for him to have a look at it. We agreed to wait until the morning to make a final call on it. I didn't get much sleep, and at 7 a.m. I got up and went for a jog around the block. I did two laps in my Swans shorts and t-shirt, and after a slow start my knee warmed up. For me that was enough. I was right to play.

On the way home I decided to call in to the corner store and get some milk and the papers.

'What are you doing?' The shop owner was into me straight away. 'Why are you running? Are you playing?'

I was a bit taken aback by the interrogation, but I told him I'd be at the SCG later that day. 'Yeah, yeah. I'm fine,' I said.

When I got home I immediately rang Gibbsy. He was very worried about the whole thing and had told me that if I got a major knock to the knee while it was in this state, it could be career threatening. 'I'm up for it' was my simple message to the club doctor.

The key to coming back from an injury is not thinking about it when you're out on the field. Once you run across that white line you have to convince yourself that everything is 100 per cent so that you play naturally. I think that was one of my biggest strengths. I could train my mind to forget that I'd come back from a serious knee injury in just two weeks when I should have been out for two months. What I was more worried about was getting the boys fired up, given that our season was on the line. With just three wins from seven games we'd slipped to eleventh position, while Port Adelaide were on top of the ladder, having lost just one game.

It felt like I had a mattress on my knee when I ran out because of the amount of taping the medical staff had wrapped around it. We got off to a flyer, kicking six goals in the first quarter, and I got involved early, which did wonders for my confidence. I even did a sidestep, which wasn't the smartest thing to do, but my knee didn't buckle, so from that point on it was full throttle. We led by five goals at half-time and maintained that advantage to the end. I finished with a game-high twenty-five possessions but was just as excited about the way we'd played. It had been like the Sydney of 2005 and 2006.

Everyone was pumped afterwards, and my unexpected comeback was the hot topic. 'He's so mentally tough, and he's probably a fair bit sorer than what he let on to the medical staff,' Roosy said in the post-match media conference. 'He's become a genuine star of the competition. There's not many guys who could do what he did today.'

I told the reporters my secret was very much a traditional Irish remedy. 'Plenty of Guinness and potatoes … Oh, the doctor won't like that. No, I'm lucky. I suppose I'm just a quick healer. I think when you're out injured you just miss being with the boys and you miss playing. You don't like being out. When they lose you feel for them and you want to get back as quickly as possible – not for yourself, but to help the boys out. At the time the injury first happens the first thing you think about is your season is gone. Once the initial fear was gone, straight away all I was thinking about was getting back.'

CHAPTER 16

I didn't know what was happening, but something was seriously wrong. My head felt like it was going to explode. I was sweating profusely and going from feeling very hot to very cold. It was the Wednesday night after my comeback game, and the fact that there was no one else at home was not helping my cause. I thought it was too late to ring Gibbsy and that a bit of sleep might help.

Oh my God. I'm going to die.

I had just woken up, and my headache had gone to another level. I'd never experienced anything like it. It was 100 times worse than a hangover headache. A stab of pain went through my head with every step I took. Then I started vomiting. I couldn't stop.

This is fucking serious.

I got hold of Gibbsy next morning and he initially thought it was flu. 'I'm telling you, Gibbsy, it's not flu,' I said. 'I need to see you. I'm fucked.'

I had to put sunglasses on as I drove to Gibbsy's because the sunlight was excruciating. I don't know how I got there because it I felt like I was lapsing in and out of consciousness because of the pain every time I went over a speed bump.

My doctor took one look at me and said, 'Quick, we've got to get you to hospital.' He asked if I had a rash anywhere, and I did, on my back. 'Oh fuck. I think it's meningitis, and that can kill you within twenty-four hours.'

Although my brain was fried, I tried to compute what he'd just said. I didn't want to die.

There was a lot of commotion going on around me when I arrived at the hospital. I was put in an isolation wing, where only people dressed in white spacesuits could come into my room. I was now very much shitting myself.

They had to do a lumbar puncture to drain fluid from my brain through my spine. The doctor who was doing it said, 'If you move, you will be crippled for life.' At that stage I didn't care. All I wanted was the pain in my head to go away. I kept my sunglasses on throughout my stay in hospital because light was my number-one enemy.

Finally, I got some good news, with my test results revealing that I had viral meningitis and not bacterial meningitis, which was the kind that could have killed me within twenty-four hours. Doyley came to see me, and he had no idea of the seriousness of the situation until he was told he'd have to wear a spacesuit if he wanted to enter my room.

I told Phil Mullen that I didn't want Mum to find out because she would be beside herself. I'd tell her all about it once I'd fully recovered. I thought it was a foolproof plan, but unfortunately it didn't turn out that way. Phil missed a call from Ireland. He thought it was Mum and that she was trying to contact him because she'd found out what was going on. He rang her, but it turned out that she hadn't rung him. It had been a mate of his who was in Ireland at the time. By that stage Phil knew he had to tell Mum what was going on. She freaked out, which is an understandable response when you hear the word 'meningitis'.

I also called Nicole, which was significant because we'd broken up during my anti-Australia phase. But I just felt like I needed to hear her voice. She was shocked, as everyone was, by my latest scare, but then quite rightly pointed out that my run of bad luck with injuries and illness had all coincided with her departure from my life. She had a good point!

Gibbsy said I'd probably become sick because I'd pushed my body too far in coming back from my knee injury. I didn't play that weekend against the Western Bulldogs but declared myself fit again the following week and played in our one-point loss to Essendon at the SCG. My knee was continually swelling up, and I got a knock on it early in the round eleven game against Hawthorn. This time they called it deep bone bruising, and I took no further part in the game.

I felt like everything was unravelling. I'd lost almost ten kilograms following my meningitis scare and because of the stress caused by my knee injury. The club actually considered sending me home to Ireland just to get my mind and body right. My knee was blowing up massively and it was as big as my quad after each training session or game. I was having needles poked into it on almost a daily basis to drain fluid.

There was a hole in my knee where my kneecap had dislocated and chipped the bone, so all the fluid would leak into that area and just sit there. Immediately after the needle had taken out the fluid I felt amazing, but then I'd run for half an hour and it would fill up again. The other problem was that the skin around my knee was being damaged by the number of injections I was receiving.

As a consequence, just getting physically prepared for games was a major exercise. I managed to string five together late in the season, all of which just happened to be wins, before a training mishap put an end to my campaign. I slipped on the SCG surface during a regulation drill and dislocated my kneecap again. While I tried to stay positive and talk up my chances of being fit for the finals in three weeks' time I knew I was only kidding myself. Even with my famous powers of recovery, Guinness and potatoes weren't going to fix this one. I attempted to train in the week leading up to the elimination final against Collingwood, but it was a waste of time. Instead I went in and had the major surgery that I probably should have had earlier in the year. The season had been a disaster, and it ended on a sour note for the Swans as well, losing by thirty-eight points to the Magpies, which meant we finished seventh for the year, our worst result under Roosy.

Finding injuries had never been a problem for me, even as a kid. I broke one collarbone when I crashed my bike going down a ramp at my grandmother's when I was seven. A few months later I broke the other one when I slipped on ice as

I was walking around the car. We were at a football game, and I remember Dad was furious because he had to take me to hospital and missed the match. Sometime after that I also chopped the top of my finger off when I was changing the chain on my bike. I remember I had to pedal about two kilometres home in agony, because we always had races to see who could get back to the pub first and Noel had left me behind.

Another impressive injury happened during a school cross-country race, when I saw an opening in a wire fence that I thought would be a perfect short cut. I saw that there was a bottom wire to get over, but I didn't see the top wire so I thought I could get through. I ran up to it and jumped but right at the last second realised that the top wire was there. It was too late, and the wire got caught in my mouth, ripping out my two bottom front teeth and requiring yet another visit to the hospital.

I could look back and laugh at those incidents, but my knee injury was no laughing matter, as it had me seriously considering whether I should just pack it in and head home. I couldn't go through the year I'd just had again – it wasn't worth it. My window for going back and playing with Kerry was slowly closing. I was twenty-six now, and I couldn't wait much longer. On the flip side I didn't want to leave AFL on this note. I had started the 2007 season in amazing shape and had thought that it was going to be the year that I really imposed myself on the competition and became the superstar that Roosy had talked about. I knew I could reach that level, so thought that I should maybe give it one more go to see if it was possible.

After chatting with Noel about it he agreed that it would be madness to walk away on this note, so once again I put all my focus into recovering from the knee surgery, although I took Gibbsy's advice this time and took it very slowly. I was also buoyed by the news that the Swans had recruited another Irishman in County Carlow's Brendan Murphy. I'd heard a lot about the eighteen-year-old from Rathvilly, who was an impressive 6 foot 5 inches and by all reports had a very good engine. There had been a recent influx of Irishman into the AFL, with Carlton recruiting Setanta and Aisake Ó hAilpín from the Cork senior hurling team. Setanta, who was also a great size at 6 foot 6 inches and very mobile, had made his debut in 2005 and had established himself by playing every game in 2007. Collingwood had also found themselves a good Irishman in Marty Clarke, a skilful left-footer from County Down, who had played his first game against the Swans in round twelve at Telstra Stadium just six months after he'd picked up an Aussie rules ball for the first time.

Naturally, when our new man arrived in November I felt obliged to help him settle in, given that I knew exactly the culture shock he was about to experience. The first thing I had to do was get him some new clothes. Murph had rocked up wearing a county jersey and an old t-shirt, exactly what I'd done eight years earlier. I'd learned the hard away about fashion and what was in and what wasn't in Australia. When

I first arrived I tucked my t-shirt into my shorts or trousers, which I soon realised was the number-one fashion crime in Sydney! I also wouldn't be seen dead in pink at the start, but now I wore it all the time, much to my mother's chagrin. I was now very much the metrosexual.

Murph needed help, so on his first day at the club I took him down to one of the surf shops to deck him out in some trendy summer gear. We picked out some shorts and t-shirts before the shop attendant came over and said to him, 'Do you want some thongs?' In Ireland the word thong means a g-string. Unsurprisingly, he looked at her strangely and then came over to me.

'This bird has just asked me if I want some thongs,' he said. 'Do you wear thongs?'

I played it perfectly, controlling my urge to laugh, because I could see by his face that he was freaking out. 'Yeah, I love them.'

Murph was horrified. 'Well, fuck that. I'm not wearing g-strings.'

With that, I cracked up laughing. I went over to the shop assistant and told her about the misunderstanding. We nearly wet ourselves. Murph eventually saw the funny side and purchased a pair of Australian thongs, known in Ireland as flip-flops, which he wore on his feet.

CHAPTER 17

'You dumb fucking Irishman.'

I was screaming those words as I lay on the ground in agony after having what felt like my shoulder torn out of its socket. I couldn't believe what had just happened. It was the week before the start of the 2008 season, and I'd decided to play in a reserves practice match just to get some practice, because I'd missed most of the pre-season recovering from knee surgery.

Mentally, I also needed to try and become more confident using my knee. It had been a constant battle over the summer, and I even went and spoke to a psychologist, because my head wasn't right. I was scared that because I'd put my knee through so much trauma it wasn't going to stand up. I was petrified of it buckling if I got a knock or did a sidestep. It was weird because my strength of mind had always been one of my best assets, but now it was actually working in reverse. My mind was playing games with me, and I constantly found myself thinking about the Pickett tackle.

Going into the practice match I told myself just to cruise through, because it was only about blowing away the cobwebs.

But I am a competitive beast, and when I let the guy I was playing against get an easy kick and help set up a goal, I vowed not to let it happen again.

The next time the ball came towards us I focused on nailing him, but just as I launched at him he stepped around me. I managed to grab hold of the top of his collar, but he went one way and I went the other, with my shoulder taking the brunt of it. I couldn't believe how stupid I'd been, which was why I was screaming out when Gibbsy arrived on the scene. I thought my whole season was finished right there and then.

When we got to the physio's room, Gibbsy tried to calm me down and said we'd know more after getting some scans done the next day. It was all too familiar, and I knew even before the results came back that I'd done a number on my shoulder again. The only good thing was that I hadn't chipped the bone. If I had, I would have been required to have surgery immediately. The ligaments had been damaged and the shoulder was very loose, but Gibbsy said one option was to strap it up and see how it went in the opening game of the season against St Kilda.

He knew that if he gave me an inch I would take a mile when it came to playing with injuries, and I was particularly determined to play in round one, as I'd been added to the leadership group that season, which was a huge honour. Given the strong tradition of great leaders at the Swans, I was proud that I now had the chance to add my voice to the group. When the new eight-man leadership team – Hally,

Kirky, Leo, Goodesy, O'Keefe, Craig Bolton, Ablett and I – was announced I was asked if I had aspirations to be the first Irish AFL captain. 'Who would not want to be captain of the Sydney Swans?' I said.

I also wanted the chance to play against my good mate Schneids, who'd been traded to St Kilda after being targeted by our former assistant coach Ross Lyon, who'd taken over the senior job there the previous year. In keeping with my bizarre ability to somehow play well in my first game after injury, I collected twenty-five possessions, but it wasn't enough as we went down by two points in a low-scoring arm-wrestle at Telstra Dome. My shoulder was hanging in there, and it was pretty much business as usual for the first month or so. We won three in a row, including a thrashing of our arch-rivals West Coast. It was the first time in four years that one side had dominated the other – we won by sixty-two points at Telstra Stadium – although the Eagles had lost their captain Chris Judd in the off-season when he'd decided to return home to Victoria and play with Carlton.

Once again a clash between the Swans and the Eagles didn't pass without controversy. This time it centred around Hally who, in a moment of madness, lost his temper and landed a solid right hook onto the jaw of Brent Staker. It was an unfortunate incident and wasn't a true reflection of Hally's character off the field, but this cost him a seven-week suspension.

After a brief honeymoon period I was starting to have some problems with my shoulder. It kept popping out at training or during games, but the worst moment was when it happened while I was in bed. I was sound asleep and all the muscles around my shoulder were obviously relaxed, so when I shifted in bed it popped out and a piercing pain vibrated through my body.

'What the fuck!' I screamed out, waking Nicole in the process.

'What's happened?' she asked.

'My shoulder is out.'

'You're kidding, aren't you?'

'I'm serious. We've got to get hold of Gibbsy.'

It was 4 a.m., so naturally he wasn't answering his phone. I kept ringing and ringing, because the pain was excruciating.

'C'mon, let's go around to his house.'

Gibbsy only lived around the corner. Nicole drove and I continued to cry out in pain. The thing with dislocations is that the pain goes away the moment the shoulder clicks back into place, but the pain is horrendous when it's out.

It looked like we would have to go to hospital because Nicole's banging on the door wasn't getting a response. 'Fucking hell, Gibbsy, where are you?' I yelled as I leaned against the car for support.

We were just about to leave when some lights went on, and he appeared at the front door wearing a pair of Rabbitohs boxer shorts. The South Sydney Rabbitohs, or the 'Bunnies' as they were also known, were the rugby league team Gibbsy had played for during the 1980s. 'What the hell is going on?' he said. 'I thought it was the cops.'

'The shoulder's gone again, doc.'

He came over, straightened me up and popped it back into place. The pain was instantly gone, and we got back in the car and went home. It was that easy. The next day I had to have yet another scan – that was the procedure every time it popped out – to see if the bone had been chipped, and afterwards Gibbsy showed me a technique I could use if I dislocated it again. It involved leaning over a table, holding my waist and then giving it a bash.

I got a chance to put it to good use not long after that when it went again while I was in bed. This time Nicole wasn't with me, but I woke Doyley up and then attempted to put my shoulder back into place myself in the kitchen. I was like Mel Gibson in *Lethal Weapon*, leaning over the kitchen bench, in the nude, trying to click it back in. Doyley was laughing his head off while I was trying to relax my body, because that was the key. It popped out so regularly during games that I even taught Leo how to put it back in for me, because the trainers or Gibbsy often took too long to get over to me. In the end I lost count of the number of times it popped out. I didn't have any alternative, because if I had surgery, my season, which I was already starting to think could be my last, was over.

That seed of doubt about my future in Australia grew significantly after the round eight game against Essendon, but it had nothing to do with my shoulder. This time it was my knee again. In a pretty innocuous incident in the second quarter I was hit, and my kneecap popped out again. As I hobbled off and lay on the ground in front of the interchange bench I was convinced I was cursed.

Fuck it. That's it. I'm done here.

I tried to put on a brave face as I watched us thrash Essendon in the second half. The boys were naturally all hyped up afterwards, but I just wanted to get out of there. I didn't want to answer everyone's questions about how I was feeling. I just wanted to be on my own.

Is it worth it any more? Wouldn't it be easier to just go home?

By the time I got home my head was a mess. I had a million thoughts going through my mind as I tried to work out why this was happening to me. I thought I'd started to turn the corner a bit. I was dealing with my shoulder and was confident it wouldn't greatly impact on my performance for the rest of the season. But I wasn't so sure about this new knee injury. I'd been in Australia for almost ten years, so maybe the luck of the Irish was running out.

I rang home and spoke to Mum, who'd become used to hearing my injury stories, but she was now as fed up as I was. 'Come home, Tadhg,' she said. 'Look what they are doing to you over there.'

I was thinking it might be the end when I went to have a scan the following day. While I was waiting I read in the papers what Roosy had said after the game, and it summed up how I was feeling. 'He needs a bionic body, Tadhg,' Roosy said. 'His body has been bashed around. He must be thinking, "Why did I come here? They don't body tackle in Gaelic football."'

Luckily, the scans were positive. I hadn't hurt the medial ligament this time and there was no bone damage. While it was pretty sore I knew it wouldn't take too long to settle down and ended up only missing one game. We then strung together four wins on the trot, but I was desperate for the midseason break, which came in round fourteen at the end of June, so I could give my body a rest.

It also gave me time to have a think about things. While I was putting on a brave face I was struggling. On top of my shoulder and knee issues I had also developed chronic groin pain, which was affecting my ability to train and prepare for games. I was starting to worry about what I was doing to my body. I didn't want to go home to Ireland a cripple and not be able to fulfil my dream of playing for Kerry and winning an All-Ireland medal.

The first person I shared my thoughts with was my brother. 'I'm just sick of this fucking thing,' I told him. 'I keep getting injured and my heart isn't in it any more. I missed six or seven years of Dad because I was over here. I don't want to miss anything like that again.'

Noel understood where I was coming from but urged me to stick out the season. 'Just get to September,' he said. 'Get to the end of the season, and then come home and we can make a decision here.'

I confided in Nicole about my feelings, which made things complicated for us given that she was established in Sydney and building a successful career as a stockbroker. The only person from the club who I told was George Stone. My former mentor now worked as the Swans' forward scout and was based in Melbourne, although he came to Sydney at least once a week. I arranged to catch up with him for lunch and he wasn't shocked to hear my confession.

'I don't want to be here,' I said.

He understood, but like Noel he urged me to get through the season. 'Just see how the year pans out, but I will back whatever you want to do,' George said.

I was also concerned by what was happening within the team. We seemed to be getting away from the Bloods culture and the style of play that had made us successful. We'd lost the trust and belief that we'd had in one another. Players were starting to flirt with form – taking short cuts, such as missing a massage or not working hard at training. On the field it was little things, such as players going for a mark when they should have spoiled by punching the ball clear when caught behind their opponents, or not nailing a tackle when they should have. That's how you lose trust and belief in each other, and when that happens it's very hard to get it back.

Obviously, the team was changing. Young players were coming in, and it takes time for them to buy into the culture. But I still felt that the focus of some of the players had shifted, with them seeking more individual success. I was also concerned about the shift in power away from Roosy and the coaches, with players having a lot more of a say in the running of the team. While empowerment of the players was the trend in the AFL, it was causing us problems. Players questioned the game style and put forward the idea of a less demanding style as we over-analysed recent losses. I was becoming increasingly frustrated, as we seemed to have endless numbers of meetings to talk about this stuff, when really we should have been putting our heads down, working our butts off and playing the hard, contested style that had been at the core of our success. In the end I went to Roosy and the assistant coaches and told them about my concerns.

After a bad loss to Collingwood in round twenty-one, Kirky and the leadership group called some brutal honesty sessions, which thankfully got everyone back on the same page. We then hammered Brisbane by ten goals in the last game of the home-and-away season to set up an elimination final against North Melbourne on our home deck.

I had played the previous month as though it was my last in the AFL. I was doing everything I could, playing through the pain, to get the most out of this time, and was averaging more than twenty possessions per game. We beat North Melbourne by thirty points to graduate through to the second week of the finals, but the improving Western Bulldogs, who ironically were coached by my first coach Rodney Eade, got hold of us in the semi-final at the MCG, and the curtain came down on our season with a disappointing thirty-seven-point loss.

Even though my heart was telling me that was the end, there was a part of me that still couldn't accept that I'd played my last game of AFL football. I was confused, but I knew I had time on my hands to make a clear decision. I also knew that I'd just had two of the most frustrating years of my life.

A few days after the season finished I had surgery on my shoulder, which they said would take four months to recover. The club decided not to operate on my groin problem, as they hoped six weeks of complete rest might help it to recover.

I delayed my return home because I was doing some TV commentary work for the International Rules series, which had been revived and was being played in Australia during October. The main reason for the resumption of the series was the fact that players who were reported during the matches could now be suspended from club games the following season in both Gaelic and Aussie rules if found guilty. This led to a dramatic decrease in off-the-ball incidents, and both matches were played in the right spirit, with Ireland winning the first by one point at the MCG and the second at Subiaco by four points. After initially being nervous behind the microphone I quickly warmed to the task and enjoyed analysing the game as it happened in front of me. After the final siren I got to go down to the field and interview one of my Kerry mates, Kieran Donaghy.

After a bit of chit-chat about the game I started to stir him up. 'I know you are a big AFL fan, and you often see me carve it up at Subiaco,' I said. 'So what's it like to play at Subiaco yourself?'

'Well, I've watched you burn it up for years, so it was good to get the chance to come out here.'

All the Irish boys were asking what I was doing, because there were always rumours doing the rounds at that time of year about a possible return home. I didn't let on where my head was at, as I knew nothing was set in stone until I got home and talked to my family.

The Swans wanted me to make a detour on the way to Ireland, as they'd booked me in to see a specialist in Germany about my groin injury. Goodesy and Craig Bolton had both been over to see the famous doctor the previous year. She'd apparently got English soccer star Alan Shearer back playing just ten days after undergoing her groin surgery.

Nicole came with me, and it was certainly not your normal everyday visit to the doctor. Let's just say that my private parts passed through a few sets of hands in preparation for the surgery. The boys had warned me that there might be some awkward moments and they were right. The guru doctor was a hard sixty-five-year-old woman, who declared that I could play in three days' time if I so desired, such was the effectiveness of her procedure.

Play what? That was still the question circling my head when I touched down in Ireland. I was fairly certain it was time to come home, but I had to suss out the lay of the land with Kerry first. Noel had got me the number of Pat O'Shea, the Kerry manager, while I was still in Oz, and I'd left him a couple of messages but hadn't heard back. Under his management the Kingdom had won the All-Ireland in 2007 but had been beaten in the 2008 final by Tyrone. However, a week after I'd tried to make contact it was announced that he was stepping down for family reasons, so I was in limbo for a while.

By the time I arrived home Jack O'Connor had been appointed to the job. I knew him well, as he'd been the manager of the Kerry Under-21 team that Noel and I had played on that had lost to Westmeath by a point. I tracked down his number and gave him a call. 'Look, I'm thinking about coming home,' I told him.

'Of course, if you're coming home, you'd be more than welcome back,' he said. He told me to give him a call when I had definitely made the decision so that he could the get the wheels in motion. If I was coming back, I would need Kerry to find me a job. Financially, what I was proposing to do was madness. Who would walk away from $500,000 – the value of the final year of my AFL contract – and into an amateur sport? However, although Gaelic footballers are not paid to play, the GAA's influence opens doors everywhere. The contacts made during a playing career ensure employment and business opportunities down the track.

It has always been that way, and I actually got a chance to see it for myself when I was eighteen, just before I left to go to Australia. I had applied to university and the Australian thing was bubbling along, but in the meantime I'd applied for a job at a bank. I soon received a phone call to say that I'd passed my aptitude test – which I never took – and an interview in Dublin had been arranged. Obviously, once they realised who I was – with the surname Kennelly – strings had been pulled. When I got to the interview there was another guy waiting there as well. He was sweating and pacing around because he was so nervous. I kept telling him to relax and I was throwing mint wrappers around the room without a care in the world. I hadn't done any form of preparation and when I got in there I just winged it.

A couple of days later I received another phone call to say I'd got the job. It was a joke. I hadn't done the aptitude test, they hadn't checked my leaving certificate and my interview had been laughable. But because I was a GAA player I got the job. It was all about PR for the bank – almost every second Gaelic footballer seemed to work in a bank. Noel did for a time, and he was put on the front desk because all the customers wanted to do was talk football.

When the word got out that there was a good chance I might return to Kerry, things started to happen in a hurry. I was told there was an opportunity to become a GAA development officer, which would involve going around to schools in Kerry promoting Gaelic football, for example by leading the kids in various exercises with the ball. This was perfect, as I'd just completed my teaching degree back in Sydney. A car dealership was also prepared to come on board as a sponsor and wanted me to drive around in their latest model.

Everything was falling into place, but Mum still refused to believe it was going to happen, given that she'd heard the 'I'm coming home this year' a few times over the journey. 'I won't believe it until I see your bag in the door,' she would regularly tell me.

I was petrified of one thing – how was I going to tell the Swans? More specifically, what would I say to Roosy? They'd been so good to me, and while I knew I was doing the right thing I still felt like I was letting them down. I'd kept in touch with Phil Mullen over Christmas and told him that I needed to catch up the day I landed. I think he smelled a rat.

It was strange getting on the plane without the feeling of emptiness I usually associated with the journey back to Australia. I always got this funny feeling, like a sickness in my stomach, the day I was scheduled to leave. Without fail it would be there, but this time there was nothing. Instead of it being nine months until I returned it was only going to be a month at the most before I was home and, more importantly, I was coming back for good.

NUALA KENNELLY

'The boys were inseparable when they were young, although as they grew up they had different friends. Noel was very quiet, but Tadhg always had loads of friends. There was always a crowd and a gang with him. He was never on his own, always the leader of the pack, with a gang following.

'From a very young age they would go up to the sports field, the two of them on their own. The newsagent down the road would say, "I saw the two boys head off this morning, and their bags were bigger than them." They'd have to climb over the wall of the sports field, because the gates would be locked.

They were eight or nine at this stage, and the bags would be full of footballs and boots that belonged to their father. On a Saturday morning especially, and if they were off school or on holiday, I always knew they were at the sports field, so I wouldn't have to look too far.

'When the Australia stuff started it was desperate. It was during the summer holidays, and he was working over at the island, at the racecourse, getting it ready for the races. Rick Barham was ringing and ringing and ringing. We went to the camp and they showed us a video. Jesus, Mary and Joseph, I knew nothing about Australian football and it was horrific. They were the worst scenarios they could have showed us. It was the worst, the hits that were in it – it was savage. I just said, "No way is he going." I had never seen anything like it, and years later Rick told me he never showed that video again.

'Tadhg had tunnel vision about it. It was in his head, and that was it. There was nothing we could do to change his mind, so we thought we had better let him go and see how it went. There was lots of door banging – it went on for weeks and weeks – as he was so determined. We were thinking he probably wouldn't stick it out and would come home with it out of his system. That was what we thought, but it turned out a little differently.

'When we went over for the first time, we first of all couldn't believe the journey. It was horrific. Tim had gone as far as London with him, and we wondered how we'd left him to go on his own. He'd never been out of the country before, and he was so green. When we did it ourselves we couldn't believe he'd done it alone – he must have been very brave. It is a daunting experience, especially for the first time. When we met everybody at the club they showed us around, and we could see they were very good to him. Phil Mullen was like a father figure, so that settled us, to see how well they were treating him.

'I went out on my own for his first game. We'd actually just been out there a couple of months before, but Tim was in hospital, so I went by myself. I arrived the morning of the game and flew out the morning after. Noel was playing in a Munster final, so I wanted to get back for that. It was hectic. It was unreal seeing him come on, and he got a great cheer from the crowd. There were lots of Irish people in the crowd, lots of Irish flags. It was really marvellous and a great achievement.

'We were nervous wrecks during the Grand Final. Timmy was shaking. He was in an awful state, and his heart wasn't great. We thought if he survived that, he'd survive anything. It was so close, down to that last kick, and we didn't hear the hooter, so we didn't know it was over. We were watching the clock, and then we eventually cottoned on that it was over, as the players were jumping up and down on each other. It was a great experience.

'He used to always say that he was coming home next year. When he said he was coming home in 2008 I said, "I won't believe it until I see your bag in the door." It was hard because he threatened to do it for many years and then always said,

"I'll give it one more year." My biggest fright was when he got meningitis. That phone call was terrifying.

'It's been great to see the boys playing together. They always played well together, always had a great understanding, and it's back. It's been ten years, but already you can see it, and I can tell you that Noel was very excited about having Tadhg back.'

Chapter 18

Don't cry. I am not going to cry.

I was trying to focus on anything but the forty players who were gathered in front of me.

Hold it together. C'mon.

'Look, boys,' I started to say before having to check myself. 'I've decided to pack it in. I'm going home.' Then I broke down.

It was torturing me to even to look at them. Roosy had made a great speech before I stood up and I could see he was now tearing up – so were some of the boys. It was very emotional. I'd spent ten years with most of these guys and I would do anything for them, but I now felt as though I was leaving them in the lurch.

'This is something I have always wanted to do,' I continued. 'My body has been against me. It's an issue that I've had over the last couple of years, and it has made the decision easier for me. I don't want to go back to Gaelic football a cripple. I want to contribute in some way.'

That was the thing that made it harder for me, because this wasn't your normal player retirement in which age and a troublesome body had conspired to bring a career to an end.

I was a player who could play AFL for another four or five years. And that's what I thought my teammates were thinking: 'What the fuck is he doing leaving us behind?'

'As most of you know I've always dreamed about going back and having a crack at it,' I said. 'That's why I'm going now. But boys, I reckon we just have to start to believe in ourselves again, because I think belief was the biggest thing we had in 2005 and 2006. Start believing in ourselves again and we'll be fine.'

I then quickly thanked a few people before throwing in a joke at the end, which I often did in sticky situations, about the Swans' football boss and whether he could find some more money to try and keep me. 'Has anyone seen Andrew Ireland? If he's got his cheque book, I'll take it off him, and maybe then I'll stay,' I said. Then the hugs started. There were tears and lots of men embracing.

My emotions were through the roof when I stepped into a press conference not long after to tell the football world I was quitting. 'I've spent ten years here, and they were the best ten years of my life,' I told the room, which was packed full of cameras and reporters. 'It has been a great ten years at the Sydney Swans, and I want to thank everyone who has been involved in my career out here. I remember how excited I was to play my first game. To have achieved what I have, to have won a Premiership with the best bunch of blokes, has just been amazing. And I've decided that if I did stay and play, I'd probably be half the player I was, because I'd be worried about getting injured.'

I was asked about how quickly I would be able to switch back to the game of my youth. 'I cannot wait to get hold of a round ball compared to that awful thing,' I joked. 'When I first came over here that oval ball was just so hard to get used to. At least the round ball bounces back up to you. But it will be difficult. It has been ten years.'

Roosy was next to me and he said he was 'absolutely convinced' I was making the right choice. 'As his coach, as his friend, I know he's making the right decision. It's unfortunate, and we're really going to miss him. He's been an icon at this club and I'm really sorry to see him go. But it's the right decision for Tadhg. We have always known that family commitments back home and also a burning desire to play for Kerry and follow in the footsteps of his late father Tim Kennelly would one day take him back.'

The final question of the press conference was the toughest. 'If the script went according to plan and you won an All-Ireland with Kerry this year, would you consider coming back?'

'I'm not closing the door on anything,' I said. And with that my Sydney Swans career of 158 games and twenty-nine goals was over.

It had taken almost a month for me to finally come clean. It had been particularly tough because I'd been forced to lie to my mates and even take part in pre-season training while I waited for Roosy to return from an overseas holiday. I wasn't doing anything until I sat down face-to-face with the man I respected more than anyone else in Australia.

The process started when I met Phil Mullen upon my return to Sydney at the start of January. I arrived back late on the Saturday night and on the Sunday afternoon I caught up with the club's welfare manager for a beer.

'We have a dilemma,' I said. 'I want to go home.'

'OK, I'm not going to talk you into or out of it,' Phil said. 'I'll listen to what you have to say, and I'll question you about it.'

We spent the next couple of hours going over everything. He kept throwing things at me, asking me if I'd thought about this or that. In the end he was satisfied I had all the answers.

Next on the agenda was Andrew Ireland and assistant coach John Longmire, because Roosy was overseas on a skiing holiday with his family in Aspen. They told me I needed to the talk to the senior coach.

'Don't rush into the decision,' Roosy said when I called him in the USA. 'Take a couple of days off and have more of a think about it. No one knows, so just go about it like nothing is really happening. Look, if anything it will mean you get yourself right for Gaelic footy. You can train and have the best treatment available to you.'

That was easier said than done. The boys could tell that something was up and kept asking, 'Are you OK?'

I would have to look them in the eye, guys I had gone into war with on the football field and trusted with my life, and tell them a blatant lie. 'Yeah, I'm sweet,' was my standard reply.

Doyley, who'd gone back to Adelaide the previous year after finishing up with the Swans, knew about my plans because he'd come over to visit me in Listowel for Christmas. I also eventually confided in a couple of my Sydney teammates, Hally and Monty Buchanan. 'You go and do what you've got to do,' Hally said. 'No one is going to hold it against you.'

When Roosy came back we had a series of meetings and talked about things for hours. It was the way we'd always been. I'd often go to his office to do the video review of my performance from the previous week's game, but we'd end up talking about anything but football. I loved the man and had so much respect for him that I knew this had to be handled the right way.

'I'm going to be devil's advocate,' he said at our first face-to-face meeting. 'Are you doing it for the right reason or are you doing it for someone else?'

Roosy knew it had nothing to do with money, and if the Swans had offered me a million dollars, doubling my contract, I wouldn't have taken it. He knew that I would have been insulted if they'd gone down that path. If they had, I would have walked out the door and slammed it shut, never to return. The last thing this was about was money.

In our final meeting Roosy brought his wife Tammy with him, because she understood intimately what I was going through, as she'd set up a new life in a foreign country too. We chatted about everything again before I laid it on the table for the last time.

'Right now Roosy, my heart and my drive is on the other side of the world.'

I left Australia a few days later.

CHAPTER 19

This was not how it was supposed to begin.

I was leaning against my new Opel car, which I'd only picked up earlier that day from the dealer, feeling like I was about to throw up. Noel was getting out of the other side, and he wasn't travelling much better. The problem was that we were both supposed to be running out for Listowel in an hour's time. And it wasn't just any old game. It was my first game back since I'd arrived home after quitting Aussie rules.

Everything had gone pear-shaped the previous evening when Noel came with me to Dublin as I was appearing on *The Late Late Show*. I'd only been home a couple of days and we hadn't really had a chance to catch up, so we thought we'd have a few pints after the show to celebrate my homecoming. A few turned into plenty as we made up for lost time. I didn't get out of bed at the hotel until 2 p.m., and we then had to get straight in the car for the four-hour drive home, as my comeback game started at 7 p.m.

After pulling ourselves together we walked into the clubhouse in Listowel and were confronted by a media circus. A photographer even tried to come into the changing-room with us before we abused him and shut the door. A small league game in February had never attracted such a crowd. The boys made me captain for the night, and despite my less-than-ideal preparation I busted my arse in the game and loved every second of it.

The key for me was getting games under my belt. My fitness was obviously not a concern. I just had to get used to handling the ball again, although I figured it would be just like riding a bike and everything would fall into place pretty quickly. At training I found myself trying too hard initially, in the sense that I was attempting to get involved in every play to show how keen I was. I was able to do it because of my elite fitness level, but it wasn't a smart way of doing things. I had to be more patient and get back a feel for how the game unfolds.

My return had caused a bit of fanfare, with one newspaper headline declaring 'The Crown Prince of the Kingdom Returns'. And the Kerry coaches used my return to motivate the team, because they'd won three of the past five All-Irelands and might not be as hungry for further success. It was pointed out how much I'd left behind, leaving a professional game to come home, and that for me it wasn't just another All-Ireland, which was how the rest of the squad needed to approach the 2009 season.

It wasn't all niceties though, and in one of my early games with Listowel I copped it from the crowd and on the field. The sledging was fierce, with the crowd screaming 'Fuck off back to Australia.' One player said, 'Who do you think you are coming back here for a cheap All-Ireland?'

I couldn't help stopping, looking at him and replying, 'Actually, it has cost half a fucking million dollars. How's that for a cheap All-Ireland?'

While a lot of the attention about my return focused on Kerry and the All-Ireland, another driving factor was the chance to play with Noel again. He plays at full-forward, so it's my job to feed him the ball, and it didn't take us long to pick up where we'd left off ten years earlier. We also hadn't forgotten how to have a good old brotherly barney on the pitch. In one particular game I tried to take too many players on at once and didn't slip the ball off to a teammate. 'Stop trying to take on the whole fucking team,' Noel screamed at me.

Then in the next couple of plays his opponent ran off him down the field. 'Hey, just turn around and play on your man and stop fucking letting him run down the field on his own,' I screamed.

We were standing twenty metres away from one another, launching abuse. Everyone at the ground could hear the two Kennelly boys roaring abuse at one another. Then at half-time we got into the sheds, sat next to one another and acted as if nothing had happened. Just like the good old days.

I always knew my first game with Kerry was going to be fairly emotionally charged, so I did everything in my power to play it cool in the lead-up. I'd been named on the bench for the game against Derry in Division One of the National League.

It was being played in a tiny place called Bellaghy in Northern Ireland, the complete opposite end of the country to Listowel. That didn't deter Noel, Isabelle and three of my good mates from flying up there for my big moment.

I'd managed to keep everything under control for the warm-up and the first half, but I lost it as soon as I heard the words, 'Tadhg, you're going on.' I stood up, took off my tracksuit top and then waited in the interchange box. Immediately I started to well up. It was all I'd ever wanted to do: wear a Kerry senior jersey in a game.

As I ran onto the ground I had to wipe the tears out of my eyes. Suddenly, all this emotion that had been trapped inside started pouring out. My mind was racing with different images of leaving home, winning the Premiership, losing Dad and coming back to play with Kerry. It was the weirdest feeling.

I know you're looking down on me, Dad.

I was only on for twenty-five minutes, but I loved every second of it. It felt natural, like I belonged out there. That feeling justified everything I'd been through to get to that point. The adrenalin was pumping long after the final whistle, and I was relieved that the first step towards my goal had been taken. I was a Kerry player. Now I just had to become a Kerry player with an All-Ireland medal around his neck.

Being back in the swing of things meant my opinion was regularly sought, especially regarding the age-old debate about whether Gaelic football should become professional. The short answer in my opinion is no. I don't believe it should for the simple reason that the country doesn't have enough money for the game to go professional. There aren't enough people to justify it. I mean, the population of Ireland is 4.2 million, yet Sydney alone has almost 4.4 million. TV rights are the big money-spinner for the AFL. That's where they make a lot of their money, with rival networks bidding to get the national game on their screens. We're talking hundreds of millions of dollars, and this goes a long way to supporting the professional status of the game. That type of competition among TV companies doesn't exist in Ireland. For Gaelic football to go professional it would mean turning it into a franchise sport, which would ruin the traditions of the game. You wouldn't have the traditional match-ups and rivalries of Kerry v. Cork, Mayo v. Galway or Meath v. Dublin. Instead there would be eight franchises that swallow up the county sides, and all the best players in Ireland would be divided up and attached to them.

The biggest concern for me about Gaelic football being an amateur sport is that I don't want to see people out of pocket because they are playing the game. I'm fine because I've got a job that finishes at 3 p.m., but if I had my own business, say a pub, and I had to go back and forth to Killarney by train and then play on Friday nights or at the weekend, I'd have to take half-days and continually get someone in to cover my shift. I hate to see players losing money because of their love of the game.

It's that love and pride that stands out in Gaelic football compared to Australian rules. Initially, I struggled to find a feeling for the Sydney Swans because I had so much pride and so much love for Listowel and Kerry. The culture of Listowel and Kerry is in me and will always be in me. I would often go to games with the Swans and think, 'Fuck, I wish I was going to a game with Kerry at Croke Park.'

It's very different playing a franchise sport, because you can't help but wonder whether some players are doing it for the right reasons. Money can blur the lines sometimes. I won't deny the fact that a major reason why I went out initially was for the money. I went out there to make a living. But with Gaelic football you know everyone is playing for the same reasons – everyone is playing for the pride of the parish, the pride of their family and the pride of their county. There are so many other things they could be doing. The time and effort required, at least four nights a week with a lot of travel, is a massive commitment, so you know everyone is in the same boat.

I'm not saying that it happened all the time, but there were times in Sydney when I wasn't sure if all of the players were on the same page. I worried that blokes were watching out for themselves, not playing injured in case it impacted on their career or coasting to firm up another contract. In Ireland you know blokes are going to play even if their fingers are torn off. In Australia some blokes will do that too, but in Ireland you know it's for noble reasons.

What does frustrate me is that some people think Gaelic footballers are still doing the same things they were doing twenty years ago so shouldn't be paid. That is completely wrong. Gaelic football has developed so much – players put in double the amount of time they did previously. The game is quicker and more skilful now, the training far more intense and it goes on all year round. Players should receive recognition for their commitment and that's why the player grants that the GAA give out after securing government funding in 2008 is a step in the right direction. That's not being professional; that is just a reward for effort, getting a couple of thousand euros in your pocket if you run out in a quarter-final, semi-final or final. It's not huge – I mean, it's not going to buy you a house – but at least it's something.

A retirement fund is something the GAA needs to introduce. For every year you play in the AFL you get between $12,000 and $14,000 for retirement, so if you play ten years, you walk away with $140,000 when you retire. They should have something like that in Ireland for long-serving players. Again, that is not being paid to play. It's just a thank you for years of service.

I don't share the concerns that some people have about Gaelic players being stolen by other sports. It's going to happen from time to time. It's a fact of life and there's not much you can do about it. If a player gets an opportunity to go and play a professional sport, be it Aussie rules in Sydney or soccer in London, they're going to take it. I think player drain is more of a threat in the cities, where soccer and rugby are so popular. Soccer is attractive because we are so close to England, while

Ireland's recent success in rugby will also have an effect. In the countryside, in places such as Kerry, nothing comes near Gaelic games.

I don't think that the GAA could possibly promote the game better. The football season only really goes on for four months, from June to September, and that's it. There's no real pre-season competition, like in the AFL, which means there is no presence in the media. This gives a massive free hit to soccer and rugby, who broadcast their sports almost twelve months a year and are more visible to potential players. The match between Dublin and Tyrone to celebrate 125 years at Croke Park was a perfect example of what can be done with a bit of marketing flair. It was in the middle of March 2009, and they had fireworks and a full stadium of 85,000. It was a big occasion. Although it costs money to stage such an event, that's what has to be done if the GAA wants to increase its income and attract more players.

There has been a lot of controversy in recent times about the AFL draining the Gaelic talent pool. I think it's an overreaction, given that there are only about ten Irishmen playing Aussie rules at the moment, although I think that there is potential for that number to rise to twenty in the next couple of years. But that's not that many. The problem is that there is no transparency in the drafting process. I know some AFL clubs are offering kids in Ireland, at the age of fourteen or fifteen, a couple of thousand dollars on the proviso that when they turn seventeen or eighteen they sign with that particular club. If they are approached by another club, they can't talk to them because they've already signed their rights away four years earlier. This is illegal and equates to draft tampering, but it does happen in the AFL.

AFL clubs coming over and holding camps in Ireland is a joke. That might sound silly, given that I went to a couple of camps myself before I went over to Australia, but the problem now is that they are conducted behind closed doors or by sneaking onto GAA grounds without permission. And some of the people running them are of questionable character to say the least. If an AFL club wants to have a look at these kids, they should fly them out to Australia and hold the camp over there. In the future I'd like to see a GAA-sanctioned draft camp in which twenty or so of the best young Irish players assemble to try out, with each AFL club allowed to take one, maybe two, per year. The point is that AFL teams are going to be looking to Ireland more and more over the next couple of years, when two new teams enter their competition. The GAA needs to accept that Australia is going to appeal to some junior Gaelic players, and instead of trying to stop the inevitable they should take charge of the process.

The other concern I have is that there are clubs in Australia who don't have enough resources to cater for an Irish recruit. This is the one thing I stress to all the young players who ask me about Oz. I was painted a picture of a life and I was very lucky because I got what I was promised. I was fortunate George Stone was there and that he was way ahead of his time, because if he hadn't been, I wouldn't have made it. I have no doubt about that. Marty Clarke was also lucky because Collingwood had the money to pay a coach to turn the Irishman into an AFL footballer. A lot of clubs don't have the resources to devote manpower and time to kids from the other side of the world who arrive on their doorstep not knowing a single thing about the country or the sport. That's why kids have to be so careful. I knew nothing and it was just pot luck that I ended up with the Swans in Sydney. Now I have the knowledge, I want to use it to help the next batch of potential Irish AFL players.

Gaelic footballers appeal to the AFL because of the similarities between the two codes. The key with Irish kids is that they can make the transition to the Australian code very quickly. The best thing about Gaelic footballers at eighteen years of age is that they are very fit because they've spent their entire childhoods playing a game with such a focus on running. Australian rules is now a lot more about running, although every now and then, when your time comes, you have to go in hard, with no fear, and make the ball the object, no matter what the consequences and risk being physically crunched. That's really it. Maybe two or three times a game you do that, but the rest of the time it's running, running and more running.

Ironically, it was running, running and more running that caused the first injury of my comeback. Unfortunately, a calf strain meant I had to sit out some valuable training. It also forced me to cancel a proposed trip back to Sydney for my university graduation ceremony. The Swans were also planning a lap of honour for me, as I hadn't got the chance to say goodbye to the fans. Whilst I was disappointed about not to getting back to Oz I was really more concerned about my calf and whether this was going to be the start of something all too familiar.

Chapter 20

'We're going to have to plate it. You can't play on with this.'

And with that Dr Richard Hansen turned on his heels and walked out of the room. He was going to organise the surgery for that evening on the broken bone in my right hand, surgery which would mean the end of my season and the end of my All-Ireland dream.

No way. There is no fucking way this is happening.

I chased after my doctor and stopped him.

'Hang on, hang on,' I said, 'I didn't come back from Australia to miss this chance because I have a broken bone in my hand. You are fucking kidding.'

The problem was that this was the second time I'd had this debate with Dr Hansen. I'd originally suffered the injury three weeks earlier following a mishap at training which had required minor surgery.

'What's the worst thing that can happen if I play?' I asked.

'You'll get a lump in your hand and your finger is going to lag,' Dr Hansen said.

I looked down at the hand and the fracture to the metacarpal bone on my right ring finger. 'Fucking hell, I've got nine others.'

He shook his head. 'It could be deformed.'

'So fucking what, I'll have a deformed finger, who cares? I've played with a lot worse,' I said. 'I'm telling you now, I'm playing.'

He obviously sensed my desperation and the enormity of the situation, so a deal was done. I promised to do absolutely nothing for two weeks to give the fracture as much time as possible to heal naturally.

While the calf problem a couple of months ago had turned out to be minor, this latest injury came at the worst possible time as I'd just been starting to find my feet in the Kerry team. In my first big game against Cork in the Munster semi-final on 7 June, I'd more than held my own in the 0-13 to 1-10 draw. And in the replay a week later I again had seen plenty of the ball, although it was a forgettable day for the Kingdom as we were embarrassed 0-9 to 3-10. It had been a dark day at Páirc Uí Chaoimh and the disgraceful performance meant our road to the All-Ireland would have to be through the qualifying series which didn't start for another four weeks.

After a week off to freshen up and try to get our heads around the Cork debacle, we returned to training, and it was on the first Tuesday night back that my season got turned on its head. We were doing a three-on-three drill and I had the ball in my left hand as I tried to charge through two players. One of them pushed me from behind into the other and I tripped over. I was desperate to hold onto the ball so I kept it locked into me with my left hand and put my right out to break my fall. Unfortunately, all my weight rolled over on the hand and straight away I knew something was seriously wrong. I tried to shake it off and continued on training for another ten minutes before the reality sunk in. I was in trouble.

I went to the hospital for an X-ray and you could see the fracture clearly. The next morning I flew to Dublin to see the specialist, Dr Hansen, who initially had mentioned the plate option before agreeing to put three pins into the hand. To accelerate the process I told him to just do it with a local anaesthetic, because if I had the full anaesthetic it would mean time in hospital which would cut into my recovery time. And time was something I didn't have a lot of if I wanted to keep my spot on the team.

This decision ended up being one of the most stupid things I have ever done in my life. I was wide awake and watched in horror as the doctor started chipping away at the fracture, scraping and cracking it as he tried to get it into place. The sound was sickening. From the start I went as white as a ghost and started sweating. It was surreal because I couldn't feel anything, but the noise was horrific as he drilled into my hand to put the pins in place. He'd actually asked me before the start what music I liked as he thought that might help keep me relaxed. I said either U2 or Kings of Leon, so they put on the latter and as the song 'Sex on Fire' was playing I couldn't help but think how the last thing I thought I'd be doing to this music was having open-hand surgery.

The injury forced me out of the first qualifying game against Longford which we won 1-12 to 0-11, but once again our game had been far from impressive. The next day I went for a training run with our conditioning coach, just a light kick, but somehow I managed to fall over and hurt the hand again. I was scheduled to go back to Dublin the next day to see Dr Hansen anyway, but there was suddenly a lot more urgency about the check-up.

I tried to play it cool, hoping my instincts were wrong, and decided not to tell my doctor about the training incident.

'It's just a bit sore so I think I'll probably need another X-ray to see how it's coming on,' I said.

When he saw the X-ray, Dr Hansen burst back into his office where I was waiting. 'What have you been doing?'

Two of the three pins had come out of position. I really liked my doctor, he had a good sense of humour, so I shot back at him, 'What have you been doing? All I did was catch a football and two pins came out. What the fuck is going on with your surgery?'

He laughed and returned with a barb of his own. 'I did it properly, the question is what have you been doing to your hand?'

We then had a serious chat and after I had won the plate debate, I agreed to have two weeks total rest and wear a special guard in everything I did. I would also require a pain-killing injection to play, which really wasn't an issue for me given I'd lived on the stuff at times during my career in Sydney.

All of the stress and worry over my hand almost amounted to a complete waste of time given the way we played in our second qualifying game against Sligo in Tralee. The problem with games against lower-ranked counties is you often find yourselves playing down at their level. I had seen it many times during my time in the AFL and this type of game can be very dangerous. You go into the games knowing that you can step up a gear at any time and win the game, but sometimes this attitude can bring you unstuck, which is exactly what nearly happened against Sligo.

I was sitting on the bench and couldn't believe what I was watching. Kerry had not played well and as the game ticked into its final five minutes we were, unbelievably, only two points ahead. Sligo were pressing hard and then the worst imaginable thing happened – they were awarded a penalty.

This cannot be happening. The year is finished. All the hard work, the massive changes in my life, giving up the AFL to come home. All for nothing. I can't fucking believe this is happening.

It was like I was in a trance as I watched our goalkeeper, Diarmuid Murphy, pace the line as he prepared to try and pull off a miracle save. Murphy had been around forever and is regarded as one of the best in the country, so I knew he definitely had it in him to save our season.

He did.

Somehow Murphy had guessed where the shot from Sligo's David Kelly was heading and blocked it. I was stunned but that wasn't the end of it. From the clearance, Sligo immediately got the ball back and quickly scored a point to put them within one point of us. Thankfully, a minute later the sound of the whistle rang out through Austin Stack Park. The scoreboard read: Kerry 0-14, Sligo 1-10.

The meeting was heated. Some home truths were being delivered. None of the management were present. It was just the entire playing group in the room having a much-needed heart-to-heart. We all knew we had to get our ship in order or else the season was gone. The escape a couple of days earlier against Sligo had rammed that home to all of us, but off the field we were having just as many troubles. Before the start of the qualifying series, we'd all agreed to stay off the drink for a month because we were scheduled to play on four consecutive weekends. It was a small sacrifice but one which all the players had agreed was the right thing to do. Unfortunately, two of our best players, Colm 'the Gooch' Cooper and Tomás Ó Sé had broken the ban on the Saturday night after the Sligo game. They both got up in front of the group and apologised, but the question of punishment was one which was the subject of spirited debate. Some said drop them for the next game against Antrim, while others weren't sure if that was the way to go given the circumstances we found ourselves in. Could we really afford to drop two of our best players the way we were playing?

It wasn't a case of the drink being a problem, it was the fact that we'd all said we wouldn't do it. They had gone against the team rule, broken our trust, and in the end it was agreed that both players would start on the bench against Antrim.

That wasn't the only item on the agenda at the meeting. A number of the senior players, including captain Darren O'Sullivan, Darragh Ó Sé and Paul Galvin, spoke passionately about the position we found ourselves in. We discussed the game plan, what was working and what wasn't, and suggested changes for training. Mike Quirke, a player who was a major personality in the make-up of the group, steered the meeting and was the one who had the responsibility of relaying our thoughts back to the management. The meeting lasted over an hour and even at the training session immediately afterwards I could already sense a change. We had desperately needed something to galvanise the team and I had a feeling that if we made the final in two months time we just might be looking back at the crisis talks as the turning point of the season. I desperately hoped so.

My own season was also turning around, with the hand getting the all clear in time for me to play against Antrim. I was a bit surprised to be rushed back into the starting line-up as I had been unable to train much before the match, but I came into the team along with Killian Young as replacements for Cooper and Ó Sé. I was confident that the mix of adrenalin and a pain-killing injection would be enough to ensure the hand wouldn't be an issue. Unfortunately, it wasn't.

During the match my ball-handling wasn't at its best – I was uncharacteristically fumbling, although I wasn't the only Kerry player having some problems. As a collective we were again playing well below our best. At half-time we were behind 1-4 to 1-3 and had failed to score for a sixteen-minute period in the opening half against a Division 4 team. Antrim extended their lead to two points shortly after the break before the Gooch, who had come on at the thirty-one-minute mark, started to find the mark. Jack O'Connor made a number of changes – I was taken off at the forty-fourth minute – to try and get the team going. The changes worked and a goal from Galvin in the sixty-second minute was enough to finally shrug off the boys from the Glens (2-12 to 1-10). I was a relieved man afterwards, not only because of the win, but also the fact that I had got through with my hand still in one piece. I knew I would be greatly improved by this run-out and with a full week of training behind me I would be a totally different player in following week's massive quarter-final game, scheduled for Bank Holiday Monday on 3 August, against Dublin.

For the couple of months where we were scraping through, the criticism of the team had been savage and actually caught me off guard. I had forgotten just how big the game is in Ireland and what it meant to so many people. The thing about Kerry is that every time they play, they are expected to win and not just that, but to win by a lot when it's against minnows such as Longford, Sligo and Antrim. Kerry is like the Manchester United of Gaelic football. They have been very successful throughout the history of the All-Ireland, particularly in the last few years, so when we were serving up just ordinary performances, the consensus was that this Kerry team had passed their use-by date.

But what I couldn't get over was the personal attacks and the rumours which were being spread about the team because we weren't playing well. People forget that these guys are amateur footballers, yet the fans and the media treat them as if they are Ronaldo or Brian O'Driscoll in the way they are scrutinised. They're not professionals, they have to get up each morning and go to work, yet there is this incredible pressure on everything they do. If playing for Kerry was their job then they would be fair game, but it isn't their job, they are doing it for the love of the game. That's why the shit the players had to put up with was the biggest shock of my return. I wasn't immune from it; particularly after the Antrim game the knives came out for me.

'He's not that good. He shouldn't have come back.' That was the sort of thing I was hearing. And in a place like Listowel, there is nowhere to hide. I couldn't do a thing without people wanting to talk about football and it was so full on that there were times when I didn't want to leave the house. It was crazy. A good example of this was on the same weekend that the Gooch and Ó Sé got busted for drinking. I had gone out to dinner with my girlfriend Nicole, who had come over from Australia for a two-month stay, and my brother Noel and his wife. While they were enjoying a couple of drinks, I sat there all night and drank Ribena, which is blackcurrant cordial. I deliberately did that because I knew if I drank 7-Up then people would think I was drinking vodka.

Sure enough, when I got to training, our manager, Jack O'Connor, said to me: 'You were out too weren't you?'

I was stunned and before I could answer, he added: 'But you were only drinking Ribena.'

It was such a different story to what life had been like in Sydney. When we were in trouble there, we could hide, because we really weren't held accountable for every mistake. If you played a bad game in Sydney you could wake up in the morning and walk down the street and get away with it. The secret behind the Swans' success was that the players held each other accountable, which made up for the absence of heat from outside influences like the media and supporters. In Ireland, it was in your face all the time and while I had initially enjoyed that part of it when I came home, I wasn't as thrilled about it now.

I needed to produce something big against Dublin and that was all I was thinking about as I warmed up at training on the Tuesday night when the manager called me over. I figured he just wanted an update on the hand.

'We're not going to start you this week,' O'Connor said.

My heart sank.

Fuck. This is not in the script.

'Look, your hand's not right, you were fumbly on the weekend and we don't think you're right.'

I was genuinely shocked, because while I knew I hadn't been at my best, I thought I'd still done more than enough to keep my spot in the team.

'My hand is all right now Jack,' I said. 'I'm telling you I'll be right.'

But the decision had been made. 'We'll bring you on early in the game and use your energy and legs,' O'Connor said.

And with that he walked away to organise the start of training. I just stood there and didn't know what to do.

This is bollocks!

I could feel the anger building inside me and I was out of control as training began. I just wanted to nail somebody. I was fuming. What was worse was that at the end of the session my hand felt the best it had for weeks and I'd started catching the ball confidently again. I was not a good person to be around for the few days leading up to the game. There was a lot of anger in me, but in many ways the team felt the same way, as we'd been totally written off as having any chance against Dublin.

The city boys had been flying this season and the consensus was that they would kick the shit out of Kerry. While we mightn't have been playing anywhere near our best, the one thing this team had was pride. As soon as we got into the changing-room at Croke Park, I could sense a resolve about the group which had been missing in previous weeks. This team thrived on the underdog status more than any team I had ever seen. There was also a lot of anger throughout the playing group about the way the team had been slated by outside commentators.

My intuition was right. Within the opening thirty-six seconds we had a goal on the board thanks to the Gooch and from there the floodgates opened. Everything we touched turned to gold. Dublin simply couldn't get hold of the ball because of our sublime passing. All those who had been slagging us coming into the game would later describe the first half as some of the best football they'd ever seen.

When I got the call to go on at the thirty-one-minute mark, we were already twelve points clear. As I took off my tracksuit top, assistant coach Eamon Fitzmaurice came up to me and said: 'Show us what you're made of.'

I just stared at him and said: 'I'm going to shove it up your fucking arse.'

I was like a man possessed. Instead of my normal midfield role, I was introduced as a forward, replacing Tommy Walsh, and I relished the opportunity to play in a different position. Immediately I found plenty of space and was getting the ball in good areas. By this stage Dublin were absolutely shell-shocked and at half-time the scoreline read: 1-14 to 0-3.

There was no stopping us in the second half and things continued to fall into place for me. My hand wasn't an issue and I was kicking the ball beautifully, twice sending fifty metre bombs onto the chest of the Gooch who was on fire (he finished with 1-7). We had winners all over the park with Declan O'Sullivan also particularly rampant. At the sixty-one-minute mark I got on the board myself to stretch the lead to fourteen points. Six minutes later I got the opportunity the put the icing on the cake, kicking my second point of the afternoon and the final score of the match. In the end it was a massacre – Kerry 1-24 to Dublin 1-07.

After such a hard couple of months, there was a lot of relief in the changing-room after the game. We were obviously psyched up about what was an extraordinary seventy minutes of football, but also very glad that we'd shown Ireland just what this football team was capable of. I was pleased with the way I played, grabbing more than forty possessions in just forty minutes on the pitch, in a performance which justified everything I'd done since arriving back home in January.

After six weeks without a drink, there was no holding back on the celebrations, and a few of the lads came home with me to Ballybunion for a massive party which they called 'Monday night madness'. There were 4,000 people there and we had a cracker of a night, enjoying the spoils of an unforgettable day, which should go down in GAA history as one of the most complete performances seen at Croke Park.

We had almost another month to wait before the semi-final was to be played and somewhat surprisingly our opponent was to be Meath, who had upset Mayo in the quarter-final, winning by three points. They were renowned as a very physical team and in this game the roles would be reversed, as we were now suddenly flavour of the month and would start as red-hot favourites to win the All-Ireland semi-final.

My performance against Dublin got me back into the starting line-up at centre-forward, with Tommy Walsh, who had been the Young Footballer of the Year in 2008, relegated to the bench in a move which raised some eyebrows. However,

I was raising a few of my own thanks to media reports coming out of Australia about a possible return to the AFL. It seemed that with the Swans falling out of the Premiership race, I became a hot topic of conversation in Sydney, with my former coach being asked almost daily whether I was coming back.

'We haven't factored Tadhg into our planning for next year, but if he came out and said he wanted to come back to the club then it's a conversation I would definitely have with him,' Roosy had told reporters. 'Tadhg knows the door is always open to him at the footy club and we respect him not only as a player but also as a person. Tadhg was an exceptional Irish player for the Sydney Swans because of his outstanding decision-making skills and he's the type of player that every AFL club is still looking to recruit. He's an icon of our club and he's one of my favourites of all time – people and players.'

Roosy actually rang me virtually to apologise, explaining how everywhere he went people were asking about me. He also said that if Kerry were to make the All-Ireland final then he would be on the plane over with George Stone to support me. That meant a lot, but I didn't reveal that detail when I faced the Irish press who'd got wind of all the talk coming out of Sydney about my future.

'I would never say never,' I told them. 'I emailed someone at the Swans the other day, saying I spent ten years in Sydney, and the whole time I was being asked whether or not I was going back to Ireland. So I finally go back, I'm back less than a year, and the same people start asking when I'm leaving again for Sydney. All I know is I haven't thought about it. At the moment, all I'm about is Kerry football.'

The Swans were the furthest thing from my mind as I ran out onto Croke Park for the semi-final in what can best be described as a wet and shitty day for football. I knew there wasn't going to be a repeat of the Dublin heroics; this was going to be a tough, hard slog because of the conditions and because of the opposition's style of play.

I got a couple of nice touches early and set up Paul Galvin for our first scoring opportunity, but he sent it wide. However, we didn't have to wait much longer for the scoring to start, with the Gooch drawing a penalty at the three-minute mark. He had been pulled down by Meath full-back Anthony Moyles and Darren O'Sullivan got to take the shot from the penalty spot. Despite slipping as he kicked it, the ball found the back of the net and, importantly, we had now stamped our mark on the contest.

The greasy conditions played havoc with players from both sides and consequently the standard was well down. It was chalk and cheese compared to the last time the Kerry machine had been in action. Meath didn't manage a score until the fifteen-minute mark, but then they slowly edged their way back into the contest. We seemed to have lost our radar with lots of wides being recorded and at half-time our lead was just two points (1-03 to 0-4).

There was no panic in the changing-room and O'Connor's message was simple – go long and direct. The conditions took a lot of the tactics out of the equation, so we stripped it back to basics, with the focus on getting it in quickly to Tommy Walsh who had been brought on late in the first half. And in the opening minute of the second half we followed our manager's instructions to the letter. I ran onto the ball out wide and spotted Walsh one-on-one with his opponent near the goal, so I sent a long high ball to his advantage. The kick floated perfectly over the top, with Walsh able to fly over the Meath defender and then slam home the goal.

Two minutes later Walsh got another point after an assist from the Gooch and then I got the chance to join in on the party, running onto a loose clearing kick from Meath to get my first point of the semi-final. Suddenly, in the space of five minutes we'd blown the game apart with the lead up to seven points.

I'm going to be playing in an All-Ireland final.

The game then returned to its ugly ways, with missed opportunities from both teams the order of the day. I got involved again at the sixty-fourth minute to register my second point. Meath didn't score for more than twenty minutes before making a very late flurry just before the whistle. But we were never really troubled, winning 2-08 to 1-07 to progress through to a record sixth consecutive All-Ireland final.

There was a great atmosphere in the changing-room afterwards, with our thoughts immediately turning to a re-match with Cork, who the previous week had comfortably beaten last year's champions Tyrone. I was then called out to do a TV interview after being awarded 'man of the match' by the commentators. This was a bit of a surprise given that it had been one of those hard games to find standouts, but I had had plenty of possession, although I knew there were a lot of things I could have done better. However, if you'd said to me twelve months ago that I'd be man of the match in an All-Ireland semi-final, I wouldn't have believed it in my wildest dreams.

As I made my way to the post-match press conference, I couldn't help but think how I couldn't care less who won the same award in three weeks' time, as long as it was a Kerry player. I didn't care, just as long as I had an All-Ireland medal around my neck.

'It's fantastic,' I said, when asked about my timing in regards to returning home and also getting over the hand injury. 'I don't think it has set in yet. I'm very proud after that. It's great. I put so much into coming home and it's been a success either way already, whether we win or lose.'

A lot of the questions for Jack O'Connor after the match centred around Cork and the big loss we suffered to them back in June. He was also asked about the notion that this team wasn't being treated with the respect it deserved for creating history by becoming the first Kerry team to make it to six straight All-Ireland finals.

'Of course it's hugely significant,' O'Connor said. 'It's a huge landmark for a county with the tradition Kerry has. And this team has been written off so many times and I suppose our last war cry before we went out is the fact that they were written off as far back as 2001 when they were beaten by Meath. They have been written off many years since, including 2002, 2003, 2005 and 2008, so that's a lot of days to be written off. They keep coming back. There is fierce resilience there. We are going into a final now against a right good Cork team. We feel we will give them a better game than we did in June.'

'Write us off again!' I wanted to scream to the journalists. The more people doubted us, the better we played. We'd proven that against Dublin and we were in great shape to do it again in the game that mattered the most.

This time around there were a whole lot of different circumstances when it came to a Kerry v. Cork game. The biggest and most important factor in our favour was that Cork had never beaten Kerry at Croke Park. Over the past five years the two teams had met three times at the venue and each time Kerry had prevailed. That was a massive mental advantage going into the biggest game of the year. In many ways the circumstances of our grinding victory against Meath was a perfect way for us to advance. It ensured we would go in as underdogs, it ensured that Cork would be pumped up as red-hot favourites, but there was also no doubt they would be thinking: 'Fuck, here we go, Kerry at Croke Park again.'

Our team was now totally different to the one which had been embarrassed by Cork three months earlier. One of the great moves by our coach, who had been fantastic since that initial loss in the way that he had tried different things to improve our performance, was to lure Mike McCarthy out of retirement. The thirty-one-year-old, who had retired from the Kerry team after winning the All-Ireland championship with them in 2006, had been playing locally, but was brought in for the first game of the qualifying series against Longford. His return had bolstered our defence. Moreover, midfielder Seamus Scanlon hadn't played against Cork last time because of injury, Darragh Ó Sé hadn't been fit, the Gooch hadn't been on form and I wasn't in the forward line. Plus, one of our biggest stars, Kieran Donaghy, looked like he could be a factor in the final, having been out for most of the season because of a broken bone in his foot.

When I finally got a chance to turn on my mobile phone on the way home from the semi-final, there were dozens of text messages. A lot of people had obviously watched the game back in Oz and the Swans had actually put on a special telecast at the club's social rooms. A big contingent was coming over for the final with Nicole – her brother and parents would also be making the trip. Roosy and George Stone would be the main flag bearers from the Swans although a few of my former teammates were starting to warm to the idea of coming over.

There was a lot to organise and I also had to figure out whether I should leave Listowel in the lead-up to the final given that the traditional week-long racing carnival was on. The place went berserk during the races with 20,000 people converging on my hometown. A couple of school visits might be in order to try and keep me busy because in many ways I didn't want to stop and think about what lay ahead.

I already understood how big the occasion was going to be. I knew I was living the ultimate fairytale, I knew this could be the one chance I got to fulfil my father's wish. And I knew exactly what he would be saying to me from up above right now: 'Don't let the occasion pass you by.'

Chapter 21

'Would you just shut that fucking thing up!'

I was lying on the bed watching Paul Galvin scream at the window as he paced the hotel room. It was 1 a.m. and the music from a nightclub somewhere very close by was keeping us awake. Normally, we'd be the first two down there, living it up on the dance floor, but the fact that we were playing in an All-Ireland final in just over fourteen hours meant we were desperate to get some sleep.

We'd managed to stay relaxed earlier by watching the movie *The Hangover*, which had us laughing for two hours. It was hilarious and certainly helped keep our minds off what was ahead. It was appropriate that I was rooming with Paul, as he was the person I was with the first day I walked into training with Kerry. I remember phoning him and then driving to his house so I could get a lift in with him as I didn't want to make a grand entrance by myself. I had been determined to blend in, just be one of the lads, keep my head below the radar and get on with it. I was very conscious of the possibility that I could be seen as a know-it-all who had come in from another game. Plus I also had some doubts, not about whether I could play the game again, but about whether I could get a position in what was always a strong squad.

I remember for weeks I hardly said anything, just trained and tried to earn my stripes. Eventually, as I became more comfortable and we began to play games, I came out of my shell and was willing to pass on my experiences from Australia. Jack O'Connor would often ask how we reacted to certain situations in Sydney. That was a big difference between the two codes because in the AFL you are trained for almost every scenario. If you're one point down with a minute to go, what do you do? You can train the mind to work through the options. In Gaelic football, if a goal is required in the final minute everyone gravitates towards the goal, which actually makes it impossible to score. It makes more sense for the two corner-forwards to go way out and create space, the sort of thing AFL players are taught to do.

It was fun reflecting on the past eight months with Paul, although we had to stop ourselves talking about the game too much as we'd both get too fired up. One minute we'd be talking about movies or women and then without realising it, Cork and what we were going to do to them would be dominating the conversation. The week leading up to the final had seemed to take a long time to come around. Before that we'd trained really hard for the two weeks after the semi-final victory, with lots of competitive work where we basically smacked the shit out of each other, to prepare for what would undoubtedly be a tough physical game.

I'd managed to avoid most of the festivities going on around the Listowel races over the previous week. The first couple of days had been fairly quiet and then I was out of town a fair bit as I was showing Roosy and George around the countryside. I took them to Ballybunion and had a couple of meals with them back at Killarney where they were staying. It was fantastic to see them and I was just blown away by the effort they'd made to come over for the game. Having Nicole and her parents around also helped me keep busy and every time I drove through town and saw the punters piling into the pubs, I just kept reminding myself, 'I'll have my own races next week.' If everything went according to plan, my party was going to be bigger and longer than the Listowel races.

I'd turned my mobile phone off on Thursday because it was driving me crazy. This meant I was relatively chilled by the time I got on the train on Saturday lunchtime for the traditional trip to Dublin from Killarney for the All-Ireland final. It's funny, because from the minute you meet up with all the boys again, you immediately relax. All week it had been so tense because everywhere I went people were talking about the final. As a consequence it seemed like it all I did was think about the game. But when I got together with the boys, I immediately forgot about everything because they just wanted to have a laugh and not talk about it. We played cards on the train and the mood was very relaxed. Once we got to Dublin, we went for a light run and stretch around UCD (University College Dublin) before heading to the hotel, where we had a meal and one final team meeting. There was a good feeling in the group. Thankfully, at 1.30 a.m. there was also a good feeling in our room as the music from the nightclub had stopped; sleep came very soon afterwards.

'Just stick to the plan, no matter what.' Darragh Ó Sé was shouting out instructions in the changing-room.

'Look, if it's one goal or two goals and we are six points down or whatever, let's just stick to our plan and we'll be fine because we know it works for us,' he continued.

We'd been very good at sticking to our plans over the past two games. For the final, we'd had many meetings about the tactics to use against Cork and our main focus was on their kick-outs. The midfield area was going to be crucial, so we really zeroed in on counteracting their kick-out. I featured prominently in our strategy given that I would be lining up on Cork captain Graham Canty. Setting up play from their half-back line with Canty and John Miskella was a major strength of Cork's, so we had to try and get them on the back foot and make them more worried about us than about attacking.

I also had a plan of my own which I shared with my roommate. 'I'm going to charge in and hit someone at the start.'

My theory was that I really wanted to set the tone for the game for our side. We wanted Cork to know that we were a totally different animal to the one they'd faced three months earlier.

I tried to control my fired-up state of mind during the warm-up. The atmosphere in the stadium was amazing with a sea of green and gold and red and white covering the terraces. As we did some run-throughs I managed to spot where Mum, Joanne, Nicole, Roosy and George were sitting in the crowd. I gave them a bit of a wink and wave. After a brief kick around I called over Harry O'Neill, Kerry's main masseur, to give my legs a rub. I didn't want to waste too much nervous energy so I lay on my back for five minutes and basically switched off.

It wasn't until we lined up for the parade and the lap of the playing arena that I started to zone in. By the time it was my turn to meet the Irish President Mary McAleese, my mind was racing. I was thinking about the game, every possible scenario, what if this happens, what if that happens. I was suddenly so switched on that I hardly paid any attention to the pre-game ceremony and the national anthem. I just wanted it to be 3.30 p.m. and throw-in time.

As we got to our positions I looked across at Galvin, who nodded, and then positioned myself on the line ready to race in when the referee put the ball in the air. My eyes were almost rolling around in the back of my head. I was like a raging bull.

We are a totally different fucking animal.

After a few strides I knew I'd timed it right. Cork's Nicholas Murphy had just turned slightly towards me which opened the way for my shoulder to catch him perfectly on the chin.

Cop that. It's different this time, boys.

He went down hard and referee Marty Duffy immediately blew his whistle. 'Oh, c'mon,' I said to the referee, 'that's not even a free kick.'

Cork got the free but I'd got my man. While I hadn't wanted to come in and seriously injure anyone, I was determined to make a statement and I think I achieved just that. Cork converted from the free kick, but a minute later the ball had been transferred to our attacking end where I ran onto it and struck a beautiful shot over to open Kerry's scoring.

The monkey is off the back.

The pace was frantic but Cork were the ones taking their opportunities. We were two points down after ten minutes before, out of nowhere, they scored a lucky goal. Colm O'Neill broke clear after one of our defenders slipped and his finish was impressive, hitting the top corner despite an anguished dive from Diarmuid Murphy.

Just stick to the plan.

The Gooch got stuck in and won two free kicks in as many minutes to bring back the margin to three points. The signs were good, as despite the scoreline we were plugging away and I had the sense that our time would come shortly. A very patient build-up where we controlled the ball resulted in me being able to pass the ball off to Tommy Walsh to get him on the scoreboard.

Then suddenly the game changed complexion and in the next ten minutes we went on a rampage. Points from Walsh, the Gooch and Declan O'Sullivan tied the game at the twenty-seven-minute mark. We could have easily been in front, with both Galvin and myself blowing relatively simple chances for points. I got my redemption a couple of minutes later, following a Gooch point with my second of the match to grab the lead, 0-09 to 1-04.

Cork eventually registered their first score in fourteen minutes at the thirty-one-minute mark, but we were running all over them with Tomás Ó Sé breaking forward for a wonderful point. The Gooch received a free kick for an off-the-ball incident and made the shot, before Cork got a free kick close to goal to register the final point of the first half. This left the scoreboard two points in our favour, 0-11 to 1-06.

As we marched off towards the changing-rooms I noticed that Canty was just ahead of me. I'd run him all over the place on the pitch and had managed to keep his output to a minimum. I figured a bit of gamesmanship was in order so I charged past him in the tunnel. My theory was that he would see me bursting into the changing-room and think, 'Fuck, this bloke is still flying.'

For dramatic affect, I also roared as I burst through, 'Is that all they've got? Is that all they've fucking got?'

As I sat in the changing-room I knew that we had one hand on the Sam Maguire. I felt we were in control of the game and if we kept doing what we had been doing then in the second half, Cork weren't going to get a sniff. They had already had a lot of wides, but a lot of that was because of the positions they were taking shots from and the fact that our backline was playing brilliantly.

'Just stick to the plan,' Darragh Ó Sé shouted once more as we ran out again.

The opening two points of the half were ours and it was clear the gods were with us as Murphy pulled off a brilliant save from a shot by Daniel Goulding. Then, five minutes later, something out of the blue completely floored me. The referee blew his whistle to indicate a substitution. I was walking back to our forward line and turned around to see who was coming on when I noticed my number on the electronic board.

Are you fucking serious?

I was stunned. For a moment I just stood there and glared at the sideline. What was going on? I felt I had done a lot of donkey work on Canty, had run him around all over the place and I sensed the game was about to open up. This was the time I'd been waiting for, the opportunity to really drive it home and make Canty's life a complete misery. I was about to reap the rewards of all my hard work because I knew physically I had plenty left in the tank and I'm not sure that he did.

I have him cooked Jack. Can't you see that?

I charged off the ground and up the steps, not once looking at my manager. This wasn't the way I had planned to finish my first All-Ireland final, sitting on the bench after fifty-one minutes. I was in shock and while I tried to get my head around my substitution for Donnacha Walsh, Cork scored twice to reduce our lead to just one point.

By the time Darragh Ó Sé joined me five minutes later – he'd been substituted for Kieran Donaghy – I was over it, and we both started screaming and shouting encouragement from the bench. Two points from Walsh in as many minutes and another from Tomás Ó Sé got the margin back out to four after fifty-eight minutes.

With five minutes to go our lead was still four and suddenly I became super, super nervous. Cork seemed to be continually surging forward, sending high balls into the Kerry box to try and manufacture a goal. The message came up that there would be two minutes of injury time played and immediately a name popped into my head – Seamus Darby. All I could think about was the famous Seamus Darby goal in the 1982 All-Ireland final which had stopped Kerry from winning five championships in a row. My father had been part of that great team who had let the goal through in the dying minutes when they had been two points clear.

Seamus Darby. Seamus Darby.

His name kept going over and over in my head as I watched Cork go forward again. But Tommy Griffin made an awesome catch and as soon as I saw that I got up and went down to the sidelines.

We'd done it.

A few seconds later I heard it – the sound of the referee's final whistle.

I'd won an All-Ireland medal.

It had been a dominant performance by a team that had been written off so many times throughout the season. The final scoreline read: Kerry 0-16, Cork 1-09.

We all charged onto the field and the place went crazy as the fans circled around us. I was hugging everybody and grabbed Galvin and screamed at him with sheer delight. Then something caught me off guard. I started to get emotional. Suddenly all I could think about was my father.

Some of the crowd hoisted me on their shoulders and carried me towards the Hogan Stand for the traditional presentation on the steps. The next ten minutes I will cherish for the rest of my life. The sight of my mother as I climbed the steps, the moment when I got to hold the Sam Maguire and my trademark celebratory jig on the stage.

I was lost for words as I was grabbed for a TV interview.

'I thought I would have been here well before the age of twenty-eight,' I managed to say as I quickly composed myself. 'I'm very, very lucky to come back in my first year and to reach an All-Ireland final. Personally, the years haven't been too easy over there.'

Asked how unique my achievement was, given I'd now won medals on both sides of the world, I said, 'I haven't really thought about it – I've just been thinking about my father to tell you the truth.'

On my early substitution, 'You'll have to ask Jack! No, I'd spent my money. I wasn't going to leave anything in the tank. You can't afford to on a player like Graham Canty. If I went into the game trying to save my legs, Graham would have soaked me up in the first twenty minutes. I just played my heart out as hard as I could and I was quite happy. I did my day's work and we've a lot of stars who came on and did their work and they were great.'

I went on to explain how we'd come into the final with a plan and had stuck to it despite Cork storming to a four-point lead early on.

'We had a plan and we were going to stick to it no matter what happened,' I said. 'It's the great character of the team. There's great experience and a great bunch of lads out there. There's been an awful lot thrown at them. They were knocked so much throughout the years and again this year. To do what we have done is absolutely unbelievable.'

By the time I eventually got back to the changing-room I was emotionally fried. I lingered there for a while, hiding away from the crowds because I knew over the next week I wasn't going to have a second to myself.

The party that night was as expected – massive. I caught up with Roosy and George for about half-an-hour, which was great, and shared a few pints with my brother and family who like me were emotionally exhausted. We still managed not to make it to bed until after 6 a.m., although I made sure I was up early because I had a special visit to make. My little cousin, Vincent McVeigh, was at Our Lady's Hospital for Sick Children in Dublin because he'd had a major back operation to fix a problem with his spine. I grabbed the Sam Maguire and a few of the boys and went over to the hospital. The kids absolutely loved it and Vincent had his Kerry t-shirt on as he lay in his bed. I stayed and talked to him for a couple of hours and to his brother Jamie, who was also there. He got a great surprise when his favourite player, Colm 'the Gooch' Cooper, presented him with the boots he'd worn in the final. It meant so much to me to see the smiles on the kids' faces.

We then headed back to the hotel for a couple of beers before getting back on the train. The first stop was the village of Rathmore, which was just a few yards inside the Kerry border with Cork and the first train station in the county. It was the thirty-sixth time a Kerry team had brought the trophy back home from Croke Park. We were all presented on stage with the biggest cheers for local lads Aidan O'Mahony and man of the match Tom Sullivan. My arrival came with a plea for a replay of the jig, which I happily did knowing it wasn't going to be the last time I would be breaking out into my victory dance.

Next it was on to Tralee where we were driven through the streets on the back of an open deck bus. I couldn't believe how many people had turned out to see us and it was pretty much the same when we got to Killarney, where a huge party had been planned. I found it a bit overwhelming so I grabbed a couple of the boys and we ducked out, got a taxi and went to a quiet little pub in the middle of nowhere where we could just sit and have nice chat. It was a great couple of hours, just talking about the game, and it didn't seem like we'd missed much when we got back to Killarney as the party was still in full swing.

I got the chance to catch up with Jack O'Connor and he actually brought up my early substitution. 'Look, I have watched the game and we actually took you off way too early,' the manager said.

I just laughed and told him it was irrelevant because the main thing was we'd won and I was now an All-Ireland medallist. That was all that mattered to me. However, all that seemed to matter to the press was my future, as the speculation that I would go back to the AFL had intensified on both sides of the globe since the victory.

In the end I thought the best thing to do was to give the Irish media what they wanted, so I described how my heart was with Kerry and how I felt I hadn't yet become all I could be as a Gaelic footballer. All of this is true, but the reality was I didn't know what I was going to do. There were so many factors to consider. My family, my life with Nicole, my financial future, my sense of unfinished business in Australia.

I'd been living a fairy tale for the past eight months. To come back in my first year and be part of an the All-Ireland winning team was extraordinary. It was unbelievable. If you wrote a movie script, it would be too far-fetched for it to have this perfect ending. So many twists and turns, ups and downs. As I reflected, one nagging thought kept coming back to me about my fairy tale.

Was there more to come?

AFL

A SHORT EXPLANATION

History

The Australian Football League (AFL) is the major professional national competition in the sport of Aussie Rules and is the country's biggest sporting competition in terms of membership, corporate sponsorship and attendances (ranked fourth in the world for attendances).

The league comprises sixteen teams – spread over five states of the country – which play twenty-two home and away rounds between late March and late August or early September. This is followed by a four-week finals series which culminates in two teams playing off for the Premiership in the Grand Final.

The AFL operates on a single table system, with no divisions, conferences or promotion and no relegation from other leagues.

Many of the current AFL teams date back to the beginning of the sport of Australian Rules Football, including the very first club, Melbourne Football Club (1859), a foundation

VFL/AFL club whose founders also first codified the sport in 1859. The Victorian Football League, commonly known as the VFL, started in 1897 with eight teams from the Victorian Football Association (VFA): Carlton, Collingwood, Essendon, Fitzroy, Geelong, Melbourne, South Melbourne and St Kilda. Richmond and University entered in 1908, but University disbanded in 1915. In 1925, Footscray (later known as the Western Bulldogs), Hawthorn and North Melbourne entered the competition. It remained in this twelve-team single-state configuration until 1982 when South Melbourne relocated to Sydney, New South Wales, to become the Sydney Swans.

The next phase of national expansion occurred in 1987, with the introduction of the West Coast Eagles from Western Australia and the Brisbane Bears from Queensland.

The league was renamed the Australian Football League in 1990 to reflect the expanded nature of the competition.

South Australia was first represented in 1991 when the Adelaide Crows joined the league. The Fremantle Football Club joined as the second WA team in 1995. After the 1996 season the Brisbane Bears merged with Fitzroy, creating the Brisbane Lions in 1996 and the Port Adelaide Football Club joined to maintain the league at sixteen teams.

Rules/Positions

The AFL has tight controls over the player lists of each club. Each club can have a senior list of thirty-eight players plus up to six rookie or veteran players. From 2006, up to two international rookies are also permitted. Clubs can only trade players during a 'trade week' at the end of each season and can only recruit new players through the AFL Draft. The rules for the draft have changed every few years since it was introduced in 1986, but the basic philosophy remains in that players are selected by clubs in the reverse of the order of their positions on the ladder at the end of the preceding season. That is, the club that finished last has first draft selection, then the club that finished second last. A salary cap (known as the Total Player Payments or TPP) is also in place as part of the league's equalisation policy. In 2009, the TPP per club was $7,693,750.

In the sport of Aussie rules, each of the eighteen players in a team are assigned to a particular named position on the field of play. These positions describe both the player's main role and by implication their location on the ground. As the game has evolved, tactics and team formations have changed, and the names of the positions and the duties involved have evolved too. In total there are eighteen positions, not including four interchange players who may come onto the ground at any time during play to replace another player.

The fluid nature of the modern game means the positions in football are not as formally defined as in sports such as rugby or soccer. Even so, most players will play in a limited range of positions throughout their career, as each position requires a particular set of skills. Footballers who are able to play comfortably in numerous positions are referred to as utility players.

Positions:

Full-back – has traditionally been a purely defensive role, with the aim of preventing the full-forward from marking the ball and scoring.

Back pocket – refers to a position on the field deep in defence.

Centre half-back – is considered a key position in defence. The centre half-back ideally needs to be strong, tall, fast and courageous.

Half-back flank – very similar to the back pocket position. However, a true half-back flanker is more attacking and concentrates on rebounding the ball out of the defensive 50.

Midfield – the midfield consists of the centre and two wingmen. They are seen as a link between defence and attack and possess very good kicking or hand-ball skills (usually on both sides of the body).

Centre half-forward – his role is usually the most demanding of any player on field, with a tall frame, good marking skills, strength and most importantly, athleticism, required.

Half-forward flank – stands wide of the centre half-forward and usually provides an alternative target for balls coming from the midfield.

Full Forward – main target in the forward line and usually is good at one-on-one contests with the opposition. This means he can produce mass amounts of goals in a season or match. Contests in the goalsquare require the strength and weight to be able to jostle or wrestle opponents to front position and keep full-backs at bay and not as much running is required as for midfielders. As a result, full forwards are typically both tall and powerfully built. As well as contesting marks with their strength, full forwards will try to run into space to shake off their defender and take an uncontested mark (this is known as 'leading', 'leading for the ball' or 'leading into space'). This means that the full forward needs to be fast, but only in short bursts.

Forward pocket – is designed as either a role for a second full forward (also known as a third key forward) or for players who are smaller but faster and more agile and capable of kicking brilliantly on the run (this is the more traditional forward pocket). Many forward pockets are quick thinking and opportunistic players. This means that they need to be short enough to pick up the ball after it hits the ground from a contest, think and move quickly to evade potential tackles, and kick or set up a goal.

Followers or on-ball division – the followers consist of three players; a ruckman, ruck rover and rover. They are known as followers because they have traditionally been used as players that follow the ball all around the ground, as opposed to playing in a set position. A ruckman is

> generally the biggest player on the team as he has to be able to jump to contest centre bounces or boundary throw-ins, with his job being to try and tap the ball down to his own players, in particular his rover, who is generally a small, quick player.

The equipment needed to play the game is minimal. As in other kinds of football, players wear boots with stops (known as studs in some regions) in the soles, shorts and a thick, strong shirt or jumper known as a guernsey.

The game is played with an oval ball, on a grassed pitch. A red ball is used for day matches and a yellow ball is used for night matches.

Four posts are erected at either end of the oval and are aligned in a straight line six and a half metres apart from each other. Lines are drawn on the field to mark the goalsquare and fifty metre arc (which shows fifty metres from each set of goals).

In Australian Football, there are two types of scores: a goal and a behind. Of the four posts, the two middle (and taller) posts are the goal posts, and the two outer (and shorter) posts are the behind posts. The area between the goal posts is the goal: kicking the ball between these posts scores a goal which is worth six points. Kicking the ball between a goal and a behind post scores a behind, which constitutes a single point. A behind is also scored if the ball passes between the goal posts, but is not kicked by the attacking team (e.g. it comes off the hands of either team, or is kicked by the defending team), or if the ball hits the goal post. (If the ball hits the behind post, the ball is considered to have gone out of bounds.) A rushed behind (also worth one point) is scored when the defending team deliberately forces the ball between any of the posts. This may occur in pressure situations where a defender decides that it is safer to concede one point to the opposing team rather than risk a goal being scored.

An important skill in Australian Rules Football is a mark, where a player cleanly catches (is deemed to have controlled the ball for sufficient time) a kicked ball that has travelled more than fifteen metres without anyone else touching it or the ball hitting the ground. A contested mark is when a player catches the ball among a pack of players. Taking a mark on the lead is when a player has marked uncontested and is well clear of his opponent.

A goal umpire judges whether a goal or a behind is scored. The goal umpire shows that a goal has been scored by pointing both index fingers in front of him and then waving two flags above his or her head to indicate the score to the other goal umpire. A behind is signalled by pointing one finger, and waving one flag.

The game is controlled by a number of field umpires, two boundary umpires whose main job is to conduct throw-ins when the ball leaves the field of play, and two goal umpires who judge which scores are recorded and are the official score-keepers of the game. In addition, there is an emergency umpire, who can replace any field umpire who becomes injured. Each of the eight umpires may report players, but only field umpires may give free kicks.

At the end of each season the Brownlow Medal is awarded to the best-and-fairest player in the AFL during the regular season (not including finals matches) as determined by votes cast by the officiating field umpires after each game. It is the most prestigious award for individual players in the sport.

ACKNOWLEDGEMENTS

A lot of wonderful people gave their time to help this book become a reality. First of all, I would like to thank my family, because without them none of this would have happened. The strength of my mother, Nuala, has been an inspiration, while my sister Joanne and older brother Noel have been there every step of the way as well. My numerous aunties, uncles and cousins have also been of great support throughout what at times have been a very difficult few years.

Another special person, my long-time girlfriend Nicole Noonan, has put up with a lot and been right behind me despite there being a lot of distance between us at times, while I moved to the other side of the world to fulfil my dream. My manager Michael Quinlan, of Top Dog, has been with me from my early days in Sydney and was the driving force behind this book coming to fruition. He continues to guide my career and I want to thank him for his commitment.

My Sydney Swans family is very large and much loved. I will always cherish my time with them and many have contributed to the book including Paul Roos, George Stone, Ricky Barham, Phil Mullen, Nathan Gibbs and my old housemate Stephen Doyle. I would also like to thank my Gaelic football families, the Listowel Emmets and Kerry, who welcomed me back into the fold with open arms and then gave me this amazing fairy-tale ride to the All-Ireland final.

I would also like to thank the crew at Mercier Press for all their time and effort in getting this project off the ground and making the process an enjoyable one to be a part of.

Finally, I would like to thank Scott Gullan for somehow piecing my life together and turning it into a book. It wasn't an easy task given we were mostly at opposite ends of the globe, but I appreciate the hundreds of hours he put in to make it happen. I would also like to thank his wife Tess and son Noah for their understanding and support.